YOUR

SORTED.

GET
YOUR FINANCES
SORTED!

Financial independence
for life

MARK DALTON
AND
GEOFFREY DALTON

Thorsons
An Imprint of HarperCollinsPublishers

Thorsons
An Imprint of HarperCollins*Publishers*
77–85 Fulham Palace Road,
Hammersmith, London W6 8JB

Published by Thorsons 1999

10 9 8 7 6 5 4 3 2 1

© Mark Dalton and Geoffrey Dalton 1999

Mark Dalton and Geoffrey Dalton assert
the moral right to be identified as the
authors of this work

A catalogue record for this book
is available from the British Library

ISBN 0 7225 3746 8

Illustrations by Andrew Higgins

Printed and bound in Great Britain by
Caledonian International Book Manufacturing Ltd, Glasgow

This publication contains the opinions and ideas of the authors. It is sold with
the understanding that neither the author nor the publisher is engaged in
rendering legal, tax, investment, financial, accounting or other professional advice
or services. If the reader requires such advice or services, a registered independent
financial adviser should be consulted. The strategies outlined in this book may not
be suitable for every individual, and are not guaranteed or warranted to produce
any particular results.

No warranty is made with respect to the accuracy or completeness of the
information contained herein, and both the authors and the publisher specifically
disclaim any responsibility for any liability, loss or risk, personal or otherwise,
which is incurred as a consequence, directly or indirectly, of the use and application of any of the contents of this book.

The value of shares and investments can go down as well as up.

CONTENTS

ACKNOWLEDGEMENTS

Thank you to all who, either willingly or unwittingly, contributed to this book. We'd particularly like to thank:

Dayo Atilade, Rachel Begley, Paul Begley, Amanda D'Singh, Norma Dalton, Hugh Dalton, Guy Faithfull, Bryony Glenn, Sarah Hackforth, Annabel Harford, Andrew Higgins, Gerald Hinkins, Derek Holmes, Julian Hutchings, Nigel Iverson, Rohini Jagmohan, Camilla Jorgensen, Cassie Knight, Marion Larsen, Jon Lorie, Peter McCaughey, Nathalie Man, Richard Nash, Sam Page, Hannah Shepherd, Naomi Shostak, Kate Taylor, Dawn Willoughby, Catherine Wills, Carole Tonkinson and the team at Thorsons.

PREFACE

Buying a lottery ticket is not the only way to become wealthy within your lifetime. You could try for a highly paid job, work overtime to gather some extra money, or maybe buy a dilapidated house to renovate and then sell at a gain. All of these options can come with considerable drawbacks; working excessively can have a tendency to disrupt a home life. Doing up a property can be time-consuming. On the other hand, leaving it to chance or not doing anything at all are not great options either. Not having at least some financial self-sufficiency could mean spending most of your time on that monthly wage-to-bills treadmill.

The alternative is to read this book and put its ideas into practice; then you can resume your life in the knowledge that, whatever you do, your financial situation will be 'sorted'. Providing you're earning at least an average salary, this could mean generating as much as £200,000 to £400,000 within your lifetime. This may not sound as dramatic as instantly winning the lottery, and naturally it will be accumulated over time. But having £2,000, £20,000 or £200,000 in available funds could make all the difference – and surprisingly enough, it's simple to do.

You'll notice this book isn't particularly long. We've managed to combine a father's financial expertise with a son's healthy intoler-ance for jargon. The result is a clear and concise book that can be read within the day. It distills the essential information you need to know without going into the small print; we'd rather let some other genius explain the intricacies of personal finance. If that's what you want, then pick another book off the shelf.

If, however, you want to know how to create your own financial independence – so that you can start living your life as you intended – then you've come to the right place. Read on about how Jon and Dan discover the tried and tested route of the 'Independence Fund'.

In the meantime, you can still buy a lottery ticket of course. But just bear in mind that if you do have your own 'Fund', whether you win or not eventually becomes immaterial.

Geoffrey Dalton
Mark Dalton
October 1998

1 WHY BOTHER?

FIRST IMPRESSIONS

'So what does she look like?' Dan asks as we walk in. There's a handful of people huddled over their newspapers and coffee.

It's far too early for us. We just don't function well at 9 on a Saturday morning. Of course it was Kate's idea to meet so early, but only because I insisted that we wouldn't last another week without her help. She probably thought I was joking; little did she know. So here we were; traipsing into the 'Bonaparte', a trendy wooden place with huge oak tables around the corner from where she lived.

'Two large coffees please,' I say as we step up to the counter.
'So this woman doesn't resent being dragged out to help a
couple of Bob's mates?' Dan asks.

'I don't know. I didn't really give her an option. There's no
way I want to miss out on whatever she told Bob. I thought
we should find out as soon as possible.'

'You're right there. But what makes you think she's going to
be able to help us?'

'Look at the impact her advice had on Bob. He's a changed
man. Have you ever seen him so relaxed as in the last few
months?'

'He's certainly not as anxious. And he doesn't avoid buying a
round of drinks anymore.'

'Do you remember how stressed he used to be? He's calm
about work for once. He's planning his next steps, thinking
about going back to study. He's a new man. When I
challenged him about it, he confessed that it's only since he's
chatted to this woman, that he's been able to take control of
his life for once. It all started with whatever she said.'

We wander to the back, balancing our coffees. Bob had been
in the same rut; a fair job, fair money, and fairly good
lifestyle, but not really going anywhere. He just wasn't
making any progress. He'd seen countless financial advisors
and friends to no avail. Then he met someone through work,
and she was his 'financial renaissance'. He now cheerfully
claims to have a recipe for financial independence.
Stubbornly, he refused to share it with us and insisted that we
meet with her ourselves. 'She'd do a better job than me' was
all he'd offer as explanation. So here we were. Sitting in the

Bonaparte, awaiting a complete stranger and somehow thinking, and secretly hoping, that she'd be able to resolve our ongoing financial crisis.

As we sit at a table near the back, Dan says, 'So, we're expecting this Kate to give us the one true path to financial liberation then?'

'All I know is that she's a freelance journalist. At the moment she's writing the financial page in a daily paper. I can't remember which one, though. Bob says her ideas are straightforward and simple to put into action. She doesn't confuse anybody with jargon.'

'Even he understood it. That's saying something.' Dan reflects.

I drain my coffee. Dan taps me under the table and nods to the door. A woman wearing a red coat has just walked in and is scanning the room. We are just about to resume our conversation when she walks purposefully over to where we sit and asks for me. Kate is a shock to both of us. Personal finances and attractive young women are an unlikely combination – and she'd just shattered our pre-conceptions. I recover and make our introductions.

'Kate, glad you could come. I'm Jon, this is Dan. He'd also like to hear about your masterplan for financial liberty. By the way, thanks for agreeing to meet up at such short notice.'

'I wasn't really given the option,' she answers. Dan offers to get her a coffee and disappears to the counter.

'So you work with Bob?' she asks, sitting down.

'That's right. He gave you a glowing recommendation. He calls you his "life-saver".'

'A slight exaggeration. Just a bit of common sense, and here he is telling the whole world.'

'Have you had many people ringing you for advice then?'

'Quite a few, in fact – though, none as persistent as you!' I'm about to apologize, but she holds out her hand. *'Don't worry, I'm just teasing. I'm glad to be here, in fact, as I've decided to do a series of articles in my financial column on "how to create financial independence", so these conversations will be useful. And who knows, maybe it'll reduce the number of calls I receive from friends of Bob desperate for financial advice.'*

Dan returns balancing three coffees. *'Why don't we start, then?'* she says, after a few minutes of chit-chat. *'Jon, can you refresh my memory on what you said on the phone?'*

'Well, we're looking for a simple solution to our financial problems and Bob mentioned your plan. It sounds ideal for us – a one-stop solution that doesn't need much time or effort applied to it.'

'Not that we're lazy – we just have better things to do.' Dan adds.

'Of course. Do you both work with Bob?' she asks.

'We were all at college together. I'm working with him and Dan and I share a flat.'

'Right – so your financial situation is probably very similar to Bob's, then?'

'From what I gather – we're in an identical situation; on the surface it all appears rosy and sometimes I think we can't complain. We're both on reasonable salaries and we have

*enough to get by. We can't complain about our lifestyle;
given we're in the middle of London, it isn't too bad.'*

'So what's the problem?'

*'We just don't seem to be getting anywhere – financially,
I mean. It's as if we're on a treadmill; we earn money,
pay the bills and very little is left.'*

'Nothing is left.' Dan corrects me.

*'How long could you last if you finished work tomorrow?' she
asks. I look at Dan. If I weren't lending him money, it would
probably be longer, but I'm not going to bring this up.*

*'I'd last about three months; maybe four if I took a cheaper
place to live.'*

'I have no reserves at all.' Dan confesses.

'Do you think it's the cost of living in London?'

*'Partly, but I'd be the same wherever I was.' answers Dan. 'My
problem is I don't even know where to start, or what I should
be doing. Finding the available cash to save is only the first
difficulty, I can't see what we're meant to do with it after that
– there are so many different opinions on what to do with
savings. Put it in a bank account, set up a pension plan, buy
some shares. Everyone has a different idea.'*

'Have you met with any financial advisors then?' Kate asks.

*'I have.' answers Dan. 'Not that they were particularly helpful.
The advisor I met wasn't too constructive when he saw I
didn't have much money to invest. He rambled on about
critical cover insurance and pensions. I didn't understand a
word he said, so I decided to do a literature search.'*

'You must have seen the selection of books in the shops, Kate.' I say. 'The personal finances section is always at the back, and there are only two types of book on the shelf; an American self-help book on how to become an instant millionaire or the "boring guide to personal finances" with a footnote by some financial institute. You need a PhD to understand some of the terms they use. Even then, they just tend to give options and more options. I don't have the time to work through a 400-page textbook – even if I did understand it. This is where you fit in, Kate. You write a financial column every week, so you must be able to get your head round it all.'

'That doesn't mean I'm fascinated by it,' Kate answers. 'Look – I became involved in this field when I wanted to be a freelance writer. I knew that I had to build up some savings before I launched into freelance work – it's far more insecure and I needed an emergency reserve, in case I didn't have work for a few months. I had to build up some savings to tide me over during the times when I wasn't going to have an income. As I used to be fairly undisciplined with money, doing something about my finances was going to be a major achievement. It was no longer just a question of available cash – this was my financial security at stake.'

'So how did you do it?' I ask.

'I did pretty much what you've done. I spoke to people; financial advisors, pension companies, my parents. In fact, I was very close to signing up for a comprehensive pension and life insurance plan – it seems funny now when I think about it. Then I spoke to a few friends whom I considered to be financially sorted – which isn't that easy to do when you think about it. I mean, you don't meet up and say "Hello, how are the children and how is the bank balance?", do you? To my amazement, a couple I'd known for ages had the solution I'd been looking for. They had accumulated a large sum of money on a fairly average salary. Until then, it just hadn't occurred to me that you could invest money before having saved some first. I always thought I had to horde some savings away first.'

'One financial advisor I spoke to said it wasn't worth investing until I had a few thousand saved.' Dan says.

'Ignore him, he's wrong. I discovered from these friends of mine, Ed and Susan, that you don't need to have savings stashed away before starting; you can build your savings up as you go along. But saving as they went along was only part of what Ed and Susan were doing. I sat and listened to them talk about it and by the end of the afternoon it dawned on me that I had stumbled on a blueprint of how to create serious wealth with little effort – and on a basic salary. And what was really interesting for me was the effect that this fund had on their lives. This plan gave them financial security, but it also guaranteed them significant wealth too. The effect was dramatic, and they are the first to admit it. They became less preoccupied with anything financial, they didn't stress so much about work or salary levels, they concentrated on what mattered to them; their family, their career and, in Ed's case, fishing.'

'Sounds good,' put in Dan.

'They had looked around at the financial schemes on offer, but none seemed to suit their needs; they didn't want to put *money into a pension and not see it for 40 years. They didn't want to see a quarter of their savings go to an advisor, either. Their savings had to be accessible at any time; in an emergency, if they decided to change careers or stop teaching for awhile.'*

'So what did they do?' I ask.

'Their teaching salaries weren't great, but they could easily live within their means, which meant they were able to put something aside as they worked. All this went into a personal fund which Susan christened the "Boot The Boss Fund"; all because the first headmaster they had worked for was a bit of a tyrant, and the last thing they wanted to do was be totally dependent on him for a job. Susan always maintains that her relationship with him changed when she knew that she wasn't totally reliant on him for an income.

'It started as just a reserve fund,' Kate continues, 'something to be used in case of an emergency. But they left it alone, and it accumulated to the point that they were able to use it as a source of supplementary income – when they needed it. Since then, it has grown into a large sum.'

'So how much did they generate with this fund?' I ask.

'About £400,000'. We allow this to sink in.

'From scratch?' I ask incredulously.

'From scratch. Admittedly they started fairly young and they're now about 45, so the fund must be about 20 years old.'

'I bet that changes your state of mind.' Dan reflects. 'And they were able to use the fund as they went along, too?'

'How did they do that?' I ask.

'Well, their financial security improved dramatically once the fund was up and running. They could see their savings accumulate, and this gave them greater confidence when confronted with decisions in their lives. Ed freely admits that they took decisions that they would never have otherwise contemplated. The fund provided an alternative income for a critical few months. It gave them the confidence to move to another part of the country where they were able to find more interesting jobs. They followed up their interests without worrying about the financial consequences; Susan did her Masters in the knowledge that she could easily afford the fees and the loss of income for a year. When she returned to teaching, she was able to obtain a higher salary and a far more interesting teaching position than she'd previously held.'

'They were far more flexible with the fund,' I note.

'Definitely. They had the flexibility to do what they wanted in life. But much of that flexibility came from the knowledge that it was there, if they needed it. In the main, they were wise enough to leave the fund to accumulate, and now Ed reckons they could live off the annual interest.'

'Which must be at least £35,000 a year,' I say. 'Did you set up one of these yourself, then?'

'Yes, I did. I also think it's something everyone can set up. What I learned from Ed and Susan is that with a basic salary anyone can generate a personal fund that will give them financial self-reliance and, in the long run, outright wealth. All you need is the know-how, an iota of discipline and a little patience. In fact, this is what my next article is about; financial self-sufficiency for the individual.'

'Has this fund given you more confidence, do you think?'

'It's hard to explain until you've done it yourself and can see it build up. It's somehow empowering. Now that my fund has been going for eight years, I feel far more financially secure, and as it increases, I do find myself thinking of opportunities that I know wouldn't have existed without the fund. It somehow broadens your horizons.'

'What do you mean by that?' I say.

'My freelance work. The fund has helped me to become a freelance writer. I might return to work full-time for a period, but I'm always able to step away from it; to pick and choose work – to some extent.'

'Have you actually used much of your fund, though?' Dan asks.

'Not really. I've used it to provide a supplementary income at times. In fact, I've recently taken some out for a downpayment on a new flat.'

'So it's more of a psychological boost for you?'

'It's been a combination of knowing it's there and using it when I have to. Although it does make a big difference knowing it's there. Think about it. Think about any decision you've recently had to take and ask yourself if it would have made a difference to have had £2,000, £20,000, or £200,000 behind you.'

'It's a financial buffer-zone then,' I suggest.

'If you like,' Kate answers. 'The chances are that you'll be changing careers in your life, or maybe you'll be made redundant, or want a change of pace. Whatever it is, you'll be *better placed to tackle the changes with some independent financial means.'*

'So how does this fund work, then?' Dan asks, draining his coffee.

'You're a bit eager for a Saturday morning! One thing at a time, please. I was hoping we'd at least get some breakfast before I started on that. I'm starved!'

'Same here. Let's get some breakfast. I'll get it organized.' Dan stands up, looking across the tables for a menu. Kate excuses herself to make a phone call. As soon as she's out of earshot, he leans over to me. 'Jon, you'll have to get the food in, I haven't got any cash on me.'

SUMMARY

Why bother? Because:

- 'Financial independence' is both an essential pre-requisite and a realistic objective for people starting out on the savings path today.
- Individuals who are prepared to invest part of their monthly income can generate a surprisingly large source of personal funds – their own 'Independence Fund'.
- Contrary to popular belief, investing does not have to involve high risk, extortionate commissions, punitive restrictions, special knowledge or even much effort on the part of the individual.
- Establishing an Independence Fund will not only improve an individual's financial security and flexibility, but can dramatically affect their approach to life and career.

2 INDEPENDENT MEANS

'Food's on the way.' I say, returning from the bar.

'So what do you think?' Dan asks.

'What do I think of what?'

'Of Kate – what else?'

'She seems to know what she's talking about.'

'Yeah, yeah. That's not what I mean.' He leans forward. 'Weren't you surprised when she pitched up? I mean, she's gorgeous.'

'Someone I know?' asks Kate, joining us. Dan is startled.

'I was, er ... No, I was talking about a mutual friend of ours, actually.' He recovers enough to glare at me.

'So where do we start with this fund, then?' I ask Kate, moving swiftly on.

'At the beginning, of course. You have to take the first step – which is often the hardest for people to take.'

'I know what it's going to be.' Says Dan.

'Oh really? What?'

'We're going to have to start budgeting every month.'

'Wrong.'

'We're not?'

'Budgeting has nothing to do with your fund. I don't recommend it as a way to save, either. If you're that way inclined already then that's fair enough. But budgeting plays no part in setting up your fund.'

'That's the best news I've heard all morning.' Dan says, genuinely relieved. 'So where do we start?'

INVEST IN YOURSELF FIRST

The first step towards having an Independence Fund is to take the conscious decision to 'invest in yourself'. This is where we see how committed you are. If you want to create real wealth in the coming years, you need to put aside some of your monthly income. You're going to take out your savings 'at source', *before* you have a chance to spend it. Governments have done this repeatedly with great success, it's now time you used the technique to your own advantage.

Some people describe this as a 'self-imposed tax', others think of it as a simple way to save money without the hassle of monthly budgeting. I prefer to think of it as a way of prioritizing your independence savings. Although there might not be anything remarkable in putting some of your earnings aside, it's a highly efficient way of saving money. Remember that a Fund doesn't suddenly materialize, you need to build it up as you earn by prioritizing your savings and not relying on any leftover cash at the end of the month. You don't need a lump sum to start, but you do need to commit an amount on a regular monthly basis. The easiest way to do this is to set up a standing order or Direct Debit from your bank into your Fund.

THE 10 PER CENT SOLUTION

Invariably the next question is 'how much do I have to put aside?' A good benchmark is 10 per cent of your monthly income. Now, before you start to panic, bear in mind that the amount you put aside is going to be based on your monthly earnings, so it will be different for everybody. I think you'll also find that your contributions into the Fund are going to fluctuate in line with your earnings and general expenditure. In some years you won't be able to put the full 10 per cent into the Fund. At other times, the opposite will be true, and you could be stoking up the Fund. As a general rule of thumb, 10 per cent is usually a sustainable amount that can be saved over an extended period without undue hardship.

'Ten per cent? I'd starve, Kate. I'm overdrawn at the end of the month as it is! Besides, it costs so much to live in London. You've got the rent to pay, the electricity, the gas bill, the telephone, monthly shop, the odd night out, then the tube fares, the network cards, stag nights in Blackpool, weekends in Wales, a few of the latest CDs, a night at the theatre, girlfriends ...'

'I get the point, Dan,' Kate interjects. 'Are you working at the moment?'

'Yes, I'm a chef in a restaurant in Soho.'

'So you receive a salary or wage every month? And you aren't in debt? You don't have a personal loan, credit card debts or a family to look after?'

'I'm slightly over-extended on my credit card. Otherwise I don't have a personal loan or a family to look after. Not yet, anyway.'

'I suspect you'll have no real trouble putting 10 per cent of your income aside every month. If you were a single mum living on State Benefit, then you might. But you're not – you're a young single man earning a reasonable salary and you have no dependants or major financial liabilities.'

'You say that, but I'm nearly always overdrawn at the end of the month. Maybe it's the cost of living in London, but I know I'd have trouble handing over 10 per cent of my current income.'

'Dan, listen to yourself. I'm showing you how to set up a fund that will dramatically improve your financial situation for life, but you're not sure if you can actually afford it. What if I told you that it wouldn't affect your current lifestyle at all – would you consider it then?'

Saving 10 per cent of all that you earn may seem an impossible feat right now. I know I was highly sceptical before I started, but there is only one way to find out if you can do it. Commit to putting 10 per cent of what you earn aside for four months and see what happens. I guarantee you that after four months you will have forgotten you are even doing it and you won't even notice that you're living on the remaining 90 per cent of your income. If you had been going overdrawn beforehand, you'll still be going overdrawn now – except this time you'll also be saving something. It's like a raise in your salary, except in reverse. You notice it for one month before imperceptibly adjusting to it.

Most people can live on 90 per cent of their income and put the rest aside. Many will be able to do this without a second thought. Others might have genuine problems. Remember that the 10 per cent idea is not engraved in stone and that it is more important for an individual to determine what amount they can sustain over a few years. Ultimately you need to tailor the amount to your own circumstances, but never underestimate your ability to adjust to a lower income – without any detriment to your lifestyle.

'I'm willing to give it a go. But what happens if I find it difficult to maintain?'

'If you find it difficult then reduce the monthly amount you put aside to something sustainable, but don't forget to increase it again when you can.'

'10 per cent it is,' I conclude. 'Are these savings going into a bank account?'

'No, we're going to invest it.'

INVEST THE DIFFERENCE

If you've gone to the trouble of saving part of your precious disposable income every month, you do not want to just leave it in the local bank account. The aim is to create a large personal fund for use later on in life. The route to achieve this is through the stockmarket –

though thankfully you don't need much knowledge or prior experience to benefit from investing in shares.

What you *do* need is an appreciation as to why you're going to be investing in shares – as opposed to leaving it in the bank, under the mattress at home, or using it to buy antique china dolls. The bottom line is this: You aren't going to create wealth by leaving your money in a high interest savings account. The secret is to use these savings to *generate* wealth. The aim is to invest your savings to produce the best possible return for your money.

The automatic reaction from people with little knowledge of stocks and shares is that all investing is risky. But it doesn't have to be. There are many different ways you can invest in shares. It's a bit like climbing a mountain; some routes are risky and involve climbing with ropes, crampons and pitons, while others are equivalent to a gentle stroll to the top. Investing is very much the same, and you'll be choosing a route with the lowest risk for your savings. But we'll talk about risk later on. The important point at this stage is that you understand why you need to be an investor in shares instead of a lender to a bank or building society.

'Because we can obtain a higher return for our savings,'
Dan suggests.

'That's right Dan – but do you know why?'

'Not really, no.'

'Right, then – you're going to have to concentrate for this bit, because it's critical that you understand it.' We both lean in.

When you buy shares in a company, your savings are exposed to two elements: the growth in value of that company, and a share of its operating profits. If the company is doing well, expanding, taking on new business and generally making a profit, then its share value will rise accordingly. The company's performance will translate into a rise in the value of your share price. This is referred to as 'capital growth' and reflects a rise in the underlying value of the company. The capital growth in a company is primarily responsible for the growth in your share value.

The second aspect that influences share price is the operating profit of a company. As a shareholder, you are entitled to benefit from the operating profits as well as the capital growth of the firm. On an annual basis you will receive a return from the operating profits. Part of the annual income of the company is distributed to the shareholders as 'dividends' either once or twice a year. If the company has done well, you can expect a high dividend return; if the company hasn't done so well, you can expect a lower dividend return. Capital growth and income are the two elements that will determine the return on your invested savings.

'Could you just go over the bit about the capital growth again? I'm not so clear about the difference between the capital growth and the income.'

'Think of an apple tree. You plant the apple tree in the ground. This represents your original capital – in other words, your original savings.'

'Right.'

'Now the apple tree is going to grow with the seasons. The growth in the tree is the same as your capital growth. As the tree rises and extends its branches, it changes beyond recognition from the original seedling you planted – just as

*your capital growth will no longer resemble your original
savings.'*

'Fine. I understand that.'

*'Each summer your apple tree will bear fruit. This is the
equivalent of your income – or annual dividends – that you'd
receive from a company in which you've invested. You have
two choices now: you can eat the apples or sell them. Eating
the apples is the same as drawing out your income from your
shares and spending it. Selling them instead to buy more
apple trees is the same as reinvesting your dividend for
greater growth in your investment.'*

THE EFFECT OF COMPOUND GROWTH

Now this is where it gets very interesting, believe it or not. There is a
phenomenon known as 'compound growth', which is like the yeast
in a loaf of bread. Have you ever marvelled at how a flat stodgy base
of flour, yeast and water can turn into fresh bread within the hour?
Compound growth will have a similar effect on your invested
savings, although obviously the time frame is not the same. Once
you fully appreciate compound growth, you'll never leave any
savings in a bank account again.

Compound growth results when you expose regular savings to
a repeated 'return' over time. The result is best explained visually,
which is why I've drawn this exponential curve. The phenomenon
occurs when savings are allowed to accumulate interest or capital returns over time. As your original savings accumulate with every year,
the subsequent return on your savings is going to be increasingly
higher. In time, this produces a surprising and exponential effect on
your savings.

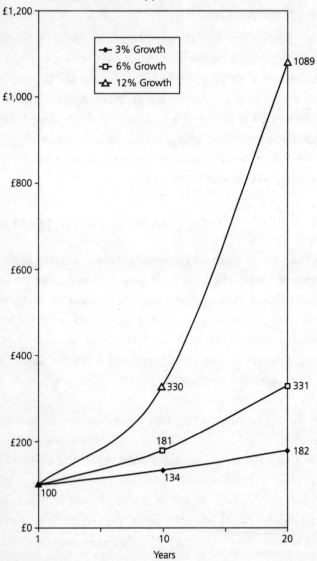

Expotential Growth Rates
£100 invested over twenty years

The graph shows the difference various returns on investment will have on £100 invested for 20 years. The 12 per cent return has produced £1,089; the 6 per cent return only £331. This is twice the return, but three times the value. This is the type of growth you want your savings to benefit from. It's impressive the way it gathers momentum – a bit like releasing a snowball from the top of a hill. As it rolls down it gathers more and more snow so that at the bottom you're left with a huge 'Swiss Roll' that has no bearing to the original size of your savings.

'I still don't understand how it works though, Kate,' I say.

'Look, imagine you invest £100 for three years. To your great pleasure you find your money has produced a return of 12 per cent by the end of the first year.'

'The combined effect of capital growth and income return?' I ask.

'That's right. So your savings has grown to £112. You leave this amount in for a second year, and again obtain a 12 per cent return. This gives you a new value of £127 that you keep invested. A 12 per cent return takes effect on £127, so that by the end of year three the total savings rises to £143.08. And so it goes on year after year, compounding all the time.'

'All from a single £100 investment.'

This compounding will occur wherever your savings are earning interest or benefiting from capital return. Savings in a bank will also be compounding; there's no denying that. But the return from a bank account comes from a fixed interest rate, typically between 2 and 6 per cent. You can see the effect of a 3 per cent return in the graph.

The growth curve is much flatter over the same 20-year period, leaving you with not much of a Swiss Roll in the way of accumulated savings. You want to aim at a much higher return on savings than that.

THE EFFECT OF GROWTH AND RETURN

Let's move on and look at the long-term effect of compounding growth. This is what underpins the success of the Independence Fund. If you can produce a consistently high return with your savings, then the cumulative effect of compound growth will do the rest. It'll convert your savings into a dramatic sum of money. One reason why people don't fully appreciate this is because it isn't so easy to calculate. Trying to work it out with a standard calculator tends to give a misleadingly low result.

Imagine you decide to invest £200 a month in the Independence Fund. Assume you put this into an Independence Fund for 20 years untouched. I know it's likely we're going to use it on the way – but for the sake of simplicity, let's keep it untouched for now. You're able to produce an average return over 20 years of 13 per cent. More precisely, your overall return for 20 years is equivalent to a 13 per cent annual return.

The results: after five years of regular payments your Fund has grown to just over £16,000. After 10 years you'll have £48,000. In 20 years' time, your savings will have accumulated to just under £230,000.

'Guess what you'd have in your Fund if you left it alone for 30 years in these conditions?'

'Over £800,000?' I answer.

'That's right. £874,653, to be precise.'

'How did you know that?' Dan looks at me, surprised.

'Kate's already written it down on the paper.'

These results are based on £200 a month. It doesn't take into account any changes in your contributions. Your earnings may increase over the years, and you may be able to put more aside in the future. On the other hand, you might also use the Independence Fund at some stage, which would affect its growth, of course. I haven't factored the effect of tax and inflation into the calculation either, although your Fund shouldn't be too adversely affected by either. This result is merely to show you what potential exists for your independence savings.

WHAT'S THE REACTION?

'It looks very impressive. But I thought the point of the Independence Fund was to see it as you go through life – not just to forget about it for 30 years,' Dan pipes up.

'We calculated this to see what impact compound growth has on regular savings. This is key to your Fund. These calculations give you an idea of the effects of compound growth on your savings if you contribute regularly and leave your Fund alone.'

'It does seem incredible that you can generate these sorts of funds through regular monthly payments. It makes me wish my parents had started a Fund when I was born. I'd be looking at over £800,000 now, just imagine that,' Dan says wistfully.

'Maybe they just haven't told you yet?' I say. 'Perhaps they're keeping it a secret until your next birthday.'

'Or maybe it never occurred to them. Or worse – maybe it did occur to them, but they couldn't be bothered.'

'Yes, that makes more sense. I'm sure it's the last one,' I offer.

'Here's our breakfast at last,' Kate says, visibly relieved. 'Are you two finished with your little daydream?'

SUMMARY

The initial steps to creating an Independence Fund are to:

- 'Invest in yourself first' by prioritizing your savings before you have the opportunity to spend them. This 'self-imposed tax' is the easiest and most effective way to save on a regular basis.

- Commit to putting 10 per cent of your monthly income aside every month. Most people can comfortably live on 90 per cent of their income. You should tailor the amount you save to your own circumstances, but do not underestimate your ability to adjust to a lower monthly income.

- Invest your savings to generate wealth and create a large personal fund. It is possible to invest with minimal risk to your savings. As an investor you will benefit from:

- a high return on your savings

- the phenomenal effect of compound growth on your savings

- the combined action of a high return on investment and compound growth, which will allow your personal fund to 'snowball' into a significant sum.

3 THE OPTIMAL ENVIRONMENT

WHAT'S IN AN IDEAL FUND?

*'I beg your pardon? You want us to tell you what the ideal
characteristics of an Independence Fund are?' Dan asks Kate.*

*'Yes. Assume you've taken the decision to put £200 aside
every month from now on. You've made a commitment to
the Independence Fund, one that should last for at least
15 to 20 years. It's a bit like a marriage; you're going to want
reassurances that you are not wasting your time or money.
So what do you think is going to make you decide that
it's worthwhile?'*

'A 40 per cent return?'

Kate rolls her eyes. 'What else?'

'But we don't know anything about investing.'

'That doesn't stop you from answering the question. If you're going to contribute 10 per cent of all that you earn into this Fund, then there must be some conditions that you'd like to see in place. You're not likely to hand over precious savings and hope that it'll just work out somehow in the end. What are the essential ingredients, if you like, that would make the Independence Fund worthwhile?'

We reflect for a moment. Kate has her pen poised as if she's about to take notes.

'I suppose the most obvious condition is a guaranteed return on our savings.'

A GOOD RETURN ON INVESTMENT

A high return on investment is never guaranteed, and your savings can drop in value as well as rise. This is the nature of investing and is of particular concern to a short-term investor who could be exposed to sudden downturns in the market. Someone investing over a number of years, who is not pressured into withdrawing their savings, will be far less exposed to market 'corrections'. Those not happy with the implicit risk of investing can always leave their savings in the local building society, with a predictable outcome: its growth will be far from impressive. Your savings will hover above the inflation rate producing rainy day savings instead of an Independence Fund.

Alternatively, if you are willing to accept a relatively low investment risk, then a much higher return on your savings is possible. In a good investment you can expect returns of between 10 and 15 per cent over a number of years, with minimal risk to your money. A reasonable target to aim for – and expect – for the Independence Fund would be about 12 per cent. This doesn't mean that you can anticipate 12 per cent for every year of your investment, it means the *average* return over a number of years should be at least 12 per cent overall. The value of your shares will fluctuate annually, altering your overall return on investment every year. If you invest for 10 years you might obtain anything between 7 and 17 per cent per annum. That your annual returns dip to 7 per cent temporarily is of no great concern, provided the average return for the entire investment period is high. In other words, an ideal and realistic return on investment is an *overall growth* in your Fund equivalent to 12 per cent per annum.

☼ IDEAL ENVIRONMENT: A return on investment of at least 12 per cent on your savings.

WHAT'S THE RISK?

Limiting the investment risk on your savings is equally essential. Risk is highly subjective and depends greatly on an individual's understanding of the share market and their financial situation. Investing can also involve very different levels of risk.

The aim for the Independence Fund is to secure a high growth with the minimum of investment risk. Your savings will be invested over the middle to long term. Short-term investing is inherently risky, as you're more exposed to fluctuations in the sharemarket. Experienced investors might argue that a higher return is possible through offshore trusts, specialized portfolios or in managing a series of short-term investments.

A private investor who has opted to manage his or her own portfolio of handpicked companies is exposed to greater investment risk. Even professionals lose serious money speculating on the market. There are people who spend their entire waking lives immersed in stocks and shares, and still don't get it right half the time. Stockbrokers are forever taking calculated risks, often hedging their investments against an unfavourable market turn. For the financially uninitiated, investing directly into the market is risky and potentially costly, and the outcome is less predictable. It can be a bit of a gamble. The Government warnings on investment advertisements – 'the value of your investments can go down as well as up' – are written with these people in mind.

The intention of the Independence Fund is that you not only benefit from high growth with minimal risk, but that you don't have to become an investment specialist in order to do so.

☼ IDEAL ENVIRONMENT: A high return on investment with minimal risk to your savings.

NO HASSLE

In addition to the attraction of high gain for little risk, the Independence Fund must be easy to set up and simple to maintain by someone with little investment knowledge. Although the Fund will require some effort on your part to set up and manage, it must be designed in such a way that it places little constraint on your time. Once set up, it will not distract you from concentrating on the more important aspects of life, whatever those may be for you.

Above all, the Fund has to be suited to the individual. A 12 per cent growth sounds far less attractive if it means you have to spend every weekend analysing the share index and making the investment decisions yourself. It should be possible to have a Fund without having to become an investment specialist.

This automatically rules out investing through a personal stockbroker, which is just as well as it is one of the more expensive routes into the stockmarket – especially if you're just starting out. This is 'high-maintenance' investing; not only do you need to monitor the share market on a regular basis, you also need to give instructions to a stockbroker whenever stocks are being bought or sold. There's also an element of skill and some luck involved in knowing when to sell or buy stocks. Some people may well be interested in being more involved in managing their shares. Bear in mind that you need time and an in-depth understanding of the stockmarket before you should start managing your own 'portfolio' of shares. More importantly, you also need sufficient funds to pay the stockbroker's fees, which means your investment will have to produce a much higher return to justify this approach. Finally, given the higher risk of investing directly into the market – which I'll talk about later – it isn't wise to invest essential savings in this way. So, unless you're an investor by profession, take a safer route into the stockmarket first; you can always play the market later on, once you have some spare capital.

An obvious way to secure a good return at a low risk is to delegate the decision-making to trusted professionals. Having someone else take the investment decisions also substantially reduces your own time commitment. The last thing you want is for the Fund to become another burden. Besides, if you're already very busy, then you simply do not have the time to dedicate to it. The optimal Fund, therefore, has to be *low maintenance* and suitable for those with little time or desire to become investment experts.

☼ IDEAL ENVIRONMENT: Hassle-free investing with no
   specialist knowledge required.

NO COMMISSIONS TO FIXERS

A major requirement of the Independence Fund is that any fees you
pay be as low as possible. There is no way of avoiding charges if you
are investing on the stockmarket as a private investor. In any case, if
you're seeking to delegate the decision-making, you will have to pay
a management fee in return, which is only fair. Still, there are
acceptable and unacceptable charges. If you're unfamiliar with the
investment world, then it is difficult to judge what constitutes an
acceptable fee. If you're not wary, you could find yourself paying an
extortionate commission for a service that you could obtain elsewhere for far less. Don't assume that a higher charge will result in a
better quality of management, either. High charges and unnecessary
commissions will severely hamper the growth of your Fund, and the
charges you pay will affect the final value of your Independence
Fund. Moreover, there is little relation between the fee you pay and
the expertise you receive. These charges need to be minimized.

Pension plans are a good example of the damage a high charge
can have on your final sum; I recently asked a financial advisor to
draft a pension plan for my retirement. I took a close look at the 'personal illustration' he presented. The one aspect that it illustrated, all
too clearly, was the rather large commission he'd receive if I had
agreed. I tentatively wondered if I should start selling pension plans –
it seemed quite profitable. Had I signed the contract, I would have
been agreeing to hand over £12,000 in charges. The bulk of this
commission was to be front-loaded; in other words, taken out in the
first 24 months of a 30-year plan. This meant that for the first two

years of the plan, only 60 per cent of my savings would be contributing to my retirement. The remaining 40 per cent was paying my financial advisor's salary.

He argued that the charges were less than 5 per cent of my overall plan, and then pointed out that my pension fund was tax-deductible and I could expect a pension fund of £250,000 by the time I was 65. He felt the charges were reasonable in this light. But he didn't mention the impact of his front-loaded commission. The effect of these deductions would rob my pension fund of an estimated £53,000 over 30 years of the plan – based on a very conservative annual growth rate. Needless to say, I declined the plan. I decided these funds could be put to better use in my Independence Fund.

Commissions of this sort are not limited to pension plans, but fortunately an Independence Fund can be set up without an initial payment to any financial advisor or third party. There will always be a management fee, however – the aim is to choose an investment route for the Fund with a very low fee. Do not underestimate the damage a few per cent in charges can do to your Fund. An ideal Fund involves no commissions and a very low management fee, making it perhaps the most cost-effective investment route available to an individual.

✵ **IDEAL ENVIRONMENT:** No commissions payable to third
   parties, and very low management fees.

EMERGENCY ACCESS

The savings in a pension plan can only be accessed once you retire, making the scheme rather impractical in the event that you need to draw out funds in an emergency before you retire. Of course, the aim of a pension plan is to guarantee funds for your retirement, so this is a justifiable condition.

The aim of the Independence Fund is to provide you with finances at important times in your life, so your savings cannot be locked away until you reach 60 or 65. You never know when you might require essential finances, and the purpose of a Fund is precisely to assist at a critical time. Whether you are acting on an opportunity or responding to a crisis, the ability to access your savings if you really need them is crucial. Without immediate access, the concept of financial independence is meaningless.

'I'm not sure how disciplined I'd be with the Fund, Kate. Depending on my financial situation, the temptation to raid the Fund could be enormous,' says Dan.

'But would you prefer a contract where you have to contribute a set amount every month, at the risk of being penalized?'

'Definitely not. The fewer contractual obligations the better. I want a flexible Fund, not a financial straitjacket. I don't need another pension plan, thanks.'

Central to the concept of the Fund is the ability to access your savings in an emergency. Of course, this places a responsibility on the individual to restrain him- or herself from dipping into the Fund needlessly. Accessing the Fund, particularly in the initial years, will stifle its long-term growth. It is wiser to allow the Fund to accumulate for a number of years and then only use it when really necessary. Self-discipline is critical, as is your perspective of what constitutes a 'financial' opportunity or emergency that is worthy of 'raiding' the Fund. Although there is scope for misuse, a Fund must be accessible as and when you need the finances. The onus is on the individual to judge when the Fund should be used.

☼ **IDEAL ENVIRONMENT:** No restrictions on accessing your savings at any time.

TAX RELIEF

A Fund should be as tax efficient as possible. Although you cannot avoid paying tax, you can minimize how much tax your savings are exposed to. Savings into an Independence Fund will be post-income tax. In other words, you've already paid tax 'at source', when you received your salary or wage packet. The only scheme which allows tax-deductible contributions is a pension plan – which, given the fact that you cannot access the funds until you retire, makes it unsuitable as an Independence Fund.

Once your savings are invested there will be little or no tax payable for many years. This is a welcome relief that allows your Fund to grow without hindrance. When you eventually do draw funds out of the Fund, you could be exposed to Capital Gains Tax and Income Tax. Although this may not sound encouraging, the real effect of these taxes is not as significant as one might expect. There are also (entirely legal) strategies that you can employ to minimize your exposure to them when you decide to draw out your funds.

Surprisingly, the scheme that offers the most favourable tax relief is not necessarily the optimal choice for your Fund. The reason for this is that tax-deductible schemes nearly always have associated charges. For a young Independence Fund, these charges are high enough to cancel out the tax benefits of the scheme. This may sound ironic, but it's true! You do not need to worry overmuch about tax relief until your Fund has reached a substantial amount. In the early years of your Fund the objective is to find a favourable tax environment where all the other optimal conditions are matched. Certainly do not accept to pay any charges in order to enter a tax-free scheme – not at this stage, anyway.

☼ **IDEAL ENVIRONMENT:** A favourable tax environment at no additional charge.

NO CONTRACTS

You do not need to sign a contract in order to set up an Independence Fund. Remember that setting up your Fund is a voluntary decision and one that has been initiated by you. The very last thing you want to do is constrain the Fund by agreeing to unnecessary charges or clauses that commit you to forced regular savings.

Fortunately, there are plenty of 'optimal choices' that do not involve any ongoing contractual arrangements and will ensure that your Fund is responsive to your needs. You need access to your Fund without having to pay penalty charges. It must be within your rights to transfer your savings if you are not satisfied with your initial choice for your Fund. Again, there should be no penalty or other unreasonable charge.

The aim of this 'I'll do it myself, thanks anyway' approach is to retain the initiative and decision-making on your own savings. Bear in mind also that choosing and setting up an Independence Fund is actually very simple, and there is little added value in asking an advisor to do it on your behalf. In fact, it is likely that an advisor will not choose the best route for your Fund. He or she will often be limited in the choice of financial products their company offers, while others may be unduly influenced by the commissions linked to particular schemes. It is probable that the optimal choice for your Fund will not be profitable for an advisor, so you can hardly expect him or her to recommend it.

The answer is to do it yourself; it's easier, it's faster and it involves less paperwork. You'll also be guaranteed of choosing an optimum environment for your Fund. We'll look at how to do this a little later on.

☼ **IDEAL ENVIRONMENT:** Maximum flexibility with no contractual obligations, commissions, penalty or transfer charges on your savings.

MOVING ON

'Right, well that's a fairly comprehensive list,' Kate looks at her watch. *'And that's good timing, too. You'll have to excuse me, but I'm meeting with some friends in half an hour. I'd better head off or I'll be late.'*

'But you haven't told us what to do yet,' I protest.

'Oh, I know, but I think we've touched on all the key points that concern a suitable investment route for your Independence Fund. Perhaps we can meet sometime next week and continue our discussion?'

'You can't leave us in suspense for that long,' Dan says anxiously. *'This is the most fascinated I've ever been about anything remotely financial. I want to find out what investment route you recommend.'*

'All in good time, Dan.'

'Look – do you have any plans for lunch tomorrow?'

SUMMARY

The optimal environment is one that will maximize savings without exposing the individual to undue investment risk, unnecessary commissions, fees or other restrictions. The ideal investment profile for the Independence Fund includes:

- a good return on your savings over the long term

- an acceptably low level of investment risk

- hassle-free investing with no special skills or insider knowledge required on the part of the individual

- no commissions or initial fees, and low management charges

- immediate access to your savings in the event of a crisis or opportunity

- minimized exposure to Capital Gains and Income Tax

- no penalty or unreasonable transfer charges on your savings if you switch to another investment.

4 THE WAY AHEAD

THE INVESTMENT ROUTE

*We live in W11, which always seems to surprise people we
meet. It's the only rented place on the road, has no number
on the door and desperately needs a paint-job. We told Kate
to look for the shabbiest looking flat in the street. She had no
trouble finding us and arrived just in time for lunch.*

*'This is nice. Very uncluttered,' Kate says, looking about
the living room, where there's a distinct lack of furniture.
'So – what's on the menu?'*

'Bangers and mash.'

'Oh? What happened to the culinary delight you promised yesterday? The only reason I finally agreed to come is because you said you were trying out a new speciality!' Dan emerges from the kitchen with a casserole dish. He's wearing his chef's hat for the occasion.

'This is a culinary delight. These are vegetarian herb sausages on a bed of new potatoes, sprinkled with spring onions and chives.'

'Vegetarian sausages?'

'We're thinking of putting them on the menu at work. You're the guinea-pig.'

Kate looks a bit wary at first, but soon the three of us are tucking in.

'So what did you get up to last night?' she asks.

'We spent the entire evening in the pub debating what investment route you would recommend,' I admit. *'Sad, isn't it?'*

'I'm impressed with your dedication. So ... what conclusion did you come to?'

'We narrowed it down to two possibilities. Obviously it is not a bank or building society account, and we're not investing directly into the stockmarket. That's too risky. It's not a pension plan – so it has to be a trust of some kind – maybe a unit trust or tracker fund?'

'Well, you're close,' Kate admits. After carefully considering all the options, I found that the ideal environment for my Independence Fund turned out to be an investment trust.'

'A what?'

WHAT IS AN INVESTMENT TRUST?

An investment trust is simply a communal pool of savings provided by thousands of investors. Each trust comprises individual shareholders who have 'entrusted' their savings to be managed professionally by an Investment Trust Management Company. This is a public limited company and is listed on the stockmarket. Instead of selling beer, computers or cars, it trades in the shares of other companies. Typically, an Investment Company might manage between two and five investment trusts.

When you buy shares in an investment trust, you become one of thousands of shareholders of that trust. The Investment Company manages the trust on your behalf. It invests your shares in a multitude of other companies, both in the UK and abroad. You become an owner of shares spread across hundreds of different companies. The size of a trust can vary from under £30 million to over £1 billion. Because you've 'teamed up' with other investors, you're able to invest across a breadth of industries and markets which simply would not be otherwise possible. This makes it a *low-risk* option because your savings are spread out over entire financial markets, as opposed to a handful of companies. It is *highly cost effective*, as the management fee is spread across thousands of shareholders.

What's the difference between an investment trust and a tracker fund?

A tracker fund *can be an investment trust. It can also be a unit trust. A tracker fund mirrors the overall performance of the stockmarket. A UK tracker fund typically shadows the overall performance of the Financial Times All Share Index, or FTSE for short. You might find a tracker fund is a good option*

*for your Independence Fund. It is also possible that you
discover a suitable unit trust for your Independence Fund,
although this is less likely. I'll explain why later on. For the
moment, let's concentrate on investment trusts.*

WHO MANAGES A TRUST?

A Management Company is appointed by the shareholders to
manage an investment trust. Fund managers are employed to direct
the investment strategy of the trusts and to take the daily investment
decisions. Their aim is to increase the value of your shares by making
the right investment decisions. A fund manager is looking for
companies that have potential for capital growth and can provide an
income for its shareholders. He or she will monitor financial and
economic indicators, watch for changes in the global markets and
specific industries, and assess individual companies before committing shareholder funds.

WHAT IS THEIR AIM?

Ultimately, trusts exist to make the shareholders wealthier. It's as
simple as that. However, the ways in which they attempt this can
vary considerably. Trusts have strict legal requirements that determine how they should be managed. Within these parameters, their
investment aims and strategies will differ. Some trusts will look to
maximize the capital growth of their fund; others will aim to produce
an income for the shareholders. Split Capital trusts will do both.
Some trusts will invest in the UK, Europe, North America, the Far
East, or Japan. Others might be international with investments
spread across global markets. Others still might specialize in particular industries, such as energy and commodities, property,

biotechnology, communications or information technology. The London stockmarket has 340 investment trusts listed, while the American equivalent, Mutual Funds, number in the thousands.

Not all investment trusts will be suitable for your Independence Fund. It is not a case of choosing just any investment trust. Not only do the aims and strategies vary – so do the associated risks and fees. You need to choose wisely. In fact, think of how you'd choose a car; there are a number of cars on the market – all different types to suit different users. You can buy a family car, a sports car, a jeep, an estate; the list goes on. It's the same with investment trusts; they've been created to suit different types of investors, and some might be highly unsuitable for your purposes. You wouldn't buy an estate to drive across the Sahara. In the same vein, you don't want to choose the wrong type of trust for your Independence Fund.

WHY AN INVESTMENT TRUST?

A GOOD RETURN WITH A LOW INVESTMENT RISK

The one major advantage of a good investment trust is that you can obtain a good return on your savings for a relatively low risk. A well-selected investment trust can produce an overall return on savings of over 12 per cent per annum. In the past, some trusts have produced returns as high as 17 per cent over 10- and 20-year periods.

This 'good return for low risk' is a benefit that comes from pooling your savings with thousands of other investors. It allows the trust to have a broad and diversified portfolio of investments, potentially across a number of regions, industries and financial markets. How broad and diversified a trust is will, of course, depend on its original aims and investment strategy. The important point to remember is that whether you invest through an international trust or an industry-specific trust, the breadth of investments will always be greater than if you had invested into the stockmarket as an individual. Your investment risk is relatively low, as the performance of your shares is linked to the performance of hundreds or even thousands of companies. In other words, your dependence on any particular industry, company or perhaps geographical region is greatly reduced.

Trusts with the lowest associated risk will be those with an international portfolio of investments, so that their exposure to any one region, market or industry is exceptionally low. With a broad-based fund, companies that are doing well compensate for the ones that under-perform. This has a 'smoothing' effect on the overall performance of your shares. A slump in one industry will not send your share price tumbling if the overall investments are stable. Equally, an impressive return on other investments could be absorbed by poorer performance elsewhere. The net result is that your shares remain fairly stable, making it easier for you to predict a reasonable return over time.

Be aware, however, that investment trusts also carry different degrees of investment risk. An international trust with investments worldwide is inherently less risky than a trust that invests solely in small companies in Southeast Asia. It would be like saying that climbing up Ben Nevis in fine weather is always safe whichever route you take. It's not. The north side has a sheer face that you'd have to rock-climb, whereas you can set off from Fort William and take a leisurely stroll up the southwest side to the summit. Two routes on the same mountain with very different levels of risk. Investing is the same. As concerns your Independence Fund, you need to find a trust that will deliver a good return with an acceptable level of risk.

DELEGATING THE HASSLE TO PROFESSIONALS

Investment trusts are extremely *low maintenance*. Many trusts have saving schemes designed for individual investors. These are generally ideal; there is a low minimum amount you have to invest, and they allow you to choose how much you wish to invest and when. Once you've decided on a trust, all you need to do is fill out a form and an instruction to your bank to transfer some savings as and when you wish.

You can invest additional funds at any time; there is no monthly minimum that you must be contributing. These schemes really are designed to be user-friendly, and they place you in the driver's seat; you decide how much, when and how. The trust company will keep you informed on how your investments are doing – normally every six months, or more regularly in some instances. The schemes make it easy for you to reinvest the income (or dividends) to maximize the growth of your savings over time.

Above all, an investment trust savings scheme need not be contractual. If you decide to stop investing or you want to withdraw your savings, then you can do so without recourse. You can access your funds at any time, usually with just a few weeks' notice. There are no penalty charges, and there are no commissions retained if you change your mind.

The other benefit is that you delegate all the investment decisions and management of your savings to the trust's Management Company. Not only are your funds in safe hands, but you won't have to spend weekends staring at the *Financial Times* trying to work out what's happening in the market. Of course, you can check the daily value of your trust by looking at its share price in the share index – but there isn't much point in doing that because you're more interested in the general trend of the fund, not whether it's up two points from last week. It's almost easier *not* to check it for a few months. So, provided you've chosen a good fund, there is very little to do apart from allow your savings to accumulate.

NO COMMISSIONS AND VERY LOW FEES

This collective approach brings economies of scale. The size of many trusts allows fund managers to negotiate lower 'dealing charges' with stockbrokers because they are trading with relatively large amounts – the pooled savings of all the shareholders in the trust. This translates into lower purchase and selling charges for the individual investor.

In addition, trusts can spread the management costs across all its shareholders, which results in a very reasonable charge to the individual. It's far cheaper than investing through a stockbroker yourself. There are typically two sets of charges you'll need to pay: an *annual management fee* and a *transaction charge*. The management fee is usually under 1 per cent of your savings, and the transaction charges will vary. Some trusts have no transaction charges; others might charge a nominal amount. A few will charge an additional 0.2 or 0.5 per cent. Total charges should not exceed 1 per cent, which makes an investment trust the most cost-effective way an individual can invest in the stockmarket today.

'*So what charges are you paying, Kate?*'

'*0.8 per cent on my invested savings and 50 pence per transaction, whether I'm depositing or withdrawing funds. That compares well with other investment options. Stockbrokers will charge about 2 per cent every time you buy*

*and sell. That would seriously start to erode a personal
portfolio of shares. Unit trusts usually have higher charges, of
about 2 to 5 per cent on your savings. The lowest management
charge I've seen was 0.2 per cent, with no transaction
charges. That's a very reasonable amount in return for
the professional management of your investments.'*

To benefit from these low fees, you do need to deal with an investment trust company directly. Don't have a financial advisor or
stockbroker arrange a trust on your behalf, as you'll end up paying
two sets of charges. An advisor will charge you up to 3 per cent on
the savings for arranging an 'equity plan', and you'll also probably be
asked to sign a contract for this privilege. This is completely unnecessary. The best way to avoid additional charges is to deal directly with
the investment trust of your choice. Besides, it is actually simpler to
do it yourself. It requires less paperwork if you deal directly, rather
than through an intermediary.

A FAVOURABLE TAX TREATMENT

An investment trust enjoys only partial tax relief, which does not
invalidate it in any way. Indeed, an investment trust savings scheme
is likely to be a better option than many tax-relief schemes on offer.

Savings into an investment trust are not tax-deductible. It is not
a pension plan where your contributions come out of your gross
income; payments will be post-income tax instead. However, once
your savings are invested there will be little or no tax payable for
many years. Having your savings exempt from tax while in the
investment trust is of critical importance. It allows the fund managers to sell stock at a profit and not have to worry about paying

high Capital Gains Taxes, which would seriously affect your returns. Now, if you had invested privately and wanted to sell your shares you wouldn't have this privilege. You'd have to pay Capital Gains Tax on any growth you'd made.

When you eventually do draw out your investment, you may be exposed to Capital Gains Tax as well as Income Tax. Although this may not sound encouraging, the real effect of these taxes is not as significant as one might expect. There are also strategies that you can employ to minimize your exposure to them when you decide to draw out your funds, which are entirely legal. Besides, you won't be exposed to Capital Gains Tax until you have about £100,000 in your Independence Fund, which makes the issue of Capital Gains Tax immaterial in the early years. This is one of the main reasons that invalidate many of the tax-relief schemes currently available, but I'll come to that later.

TO CONCLUDE

An investment trust has a number of distinct advantages which make it a particularly suitable choice for your Independence Fund. However, this doesn't necessarily mean that it is the *only* investment route for your Fund. If you assess other potential routes you may well stumble on a viable alternative. Make sure you use the 'optimal environment' and an investment trust as a benchmark for any alternative routes that you might consider. If your option fulfils all the criteria we've discussed, then the chances are you have found a suitable alternative.

I might also briefly add that the future will certainly bring change to the investment world, and investment trusts might not always be the front contenders for your Independence Fund in the future. Government legislation may bring in tax-free schemes that prove to be even better options. Competition for personal savings might also introduce new cost-effective alternatives which are currently unavailable. In the meantime, however, the investment trust is still in pole position.

HOW TO INVEST

So far an investment trust seems to fulfil all the requirements of an optimal Independence Fund environment. There is one other factor that I would like to mention here, which is not specific to an investment trust, but is related to *how you invest*. It is known officially by the rather dry name of *fixed cost averaging*. I prefer to think of it as 'bargain basement buying', which is far more descriptive.

Fixed cost averaging is a phenomenon that happens when you buy shares with a fixed amount of money at regular, say monthly, intervals. As the share price is never constant, 'drip-feeding' your savings in this way means you invariably purchase shares at different prices. When the share value is high, you buy fewer shares with your fixed sum of money. When the share value is low, you buy more shares with the same amount of money. The effect of this is that *you always buy more shares when they are undervalued*.

The great advantage of fixed cost averaging is that it automatically ensures you buy more shares when they are low, and fewer shares when they are high. This natural selection always works in your favour, as it actually reduces the average cost per share over a period of time. In other words, you're buying the bulk of your shares at a good price – when they are relatively low – hence the bargain basement analogy. As the share value rises in time, so does your return on investment. In fact, buying shares with a fixed amount of money is far more cost-efficient than to buy a set number of shares every month. To appreciate just how cost-effective this approach is, glance at the example below.

THE ADVANTAGE OF FIXED COST AVERAGING

This compares what happens when you invest a fixed amount of money as opposed to buying a fixed number of shares every month for four months. The share price for the investment trust over this period is as follows:

Month	Share Price
Jan	£2
Feb	£1
Mar	£4
Apr	£2

Example A: Investing £200 Every Month

Month	Price	Amount Invested	Shares Bought
Jan	£2	£200	100
Feb	£1	£200	200
Mar	£4	£200	50
Apr	£2	£200	100
Totals		£800	450

Average Cost Per Share: £1.78

Example B: Buying 100 Shares Every Month

Month	Price	Amount Invested	Shares Bought
Jan	£2	£200	100
Feb	£1	£100	100
Mar	£4	£400	100
Apr	£2	£200	100
Totals		£900	400

Average Cost Per Share: £2.25

I don't mean to bombard you with numbers. It's just that it is far easier to understand these things if given a visual example. This shows the effect of buying with a fixed amount of money as opposed to buying a set number of shares on a regular basis. Example A shows what happens when you invest £200 over four months. The benefits of investing with a fixed cost materialize even after this short amount of time. Your average cost per share is only £1.78 compared to £2.35, which is the cost had you bought a set number of shares every month. This is because you've actually bought 450 shares for £800 as opposed to only 400 shares at £900. This is a relative bargain of course, and this fixed cost averaging effect will occur automatically as you continue to invest on a regular basis.

Of course, I've made the implicit assumption that the share market will continue to rise in value, which means you are always buying shares at a relatively low price. But imagine the reverse happens for once, and over a period of four months the average share value drops instead of rises. Taken out of context, this at first seems like a disaster – and for a short-term investor it could be. However, provided you do not have to withdraw your savings suddenly it can work to your advantage. Remember that you are investing on a monthly basis, so you will now be purchasing shares at a relatively low price. The share value will recover and the value of your shares will rise as well. Because you've been investing on a regular basis, you've been able to purchase shares at a low price during a market slump. Provided you do not need funds immediately, a market correction is more of an opportunity than a concern, and will only be a crisis for a short-term investor.

'What if I had a lump sum to invest?' I ask.

'Dream on, Jon,' Dan says.

'You never know. I might win the lottery or get a bonus at work for my exceptional performance.'

'If you win the lottery then you need to seek expert financial advice. The same goes for any major windfall like that. Otherwise, if it's a case of a few thousand pounds and you want to accelerate your Independence Fund, then my recommendation would be that you invest the sum gradually over a few months rather than in one go,' is Kate's response.

'What's the point of that, though? Surely you want to invest it as soon as possible to maximize your return?'

'Investing it gradually over a few months lowers your exposure to an unforeseen drop in the share price. Imagine you invest £10,000 in one month. Two months later the share price drops considerably and devalues your entire £10,000. On the other hand, if you decide to feed this amount in over six months, less of your savings would be affected by the slump. In addition, you are now able to buy shares at a bargain basement rate while the share market recovers. If you

spread out your investment and there is a market slump, it can work to your advantage.'

'But what if the market is strong and there is little risk of a slump?'

'I would still be cautious and introduce a lump sum across a few months. You can rarely predict short-term corrections on the stockmarket.'

MOVING ON

'That was delicious, Dan. Remind me to leave a tip,' Kate says, pushing her plate to one side. We start to clear the table.

'That won't be necessary. Just finding out what your optimal investment route is has made this more than a fair exchange. An investment trust sounds like the ideal choice. I especially like the idea that I don't have to spend much time sorting it out. It's a very hands-off approach to investing, isn't it?'

'I thought that might appeal to you.'

SUMMARY

- An investment trust is an investment collective whereby the shareholders pool their funds to invest on the stockmarket. An Investment Trust Management Company is appointed to manage these investments on behalf of the shareholders. The primary aim of the Management Company is to improve the value of the shareholders' investments.

- It is important to choose a good investment trust for your Fund. As trusts vary in their aims, strategies and structure, not all are suitable for an Independence Fund.

- A well-chosen investment trust fulfils the optimal requirements for the ideal investment environment, making it a suitable choice for your Independence Fund. The main reasons for this are that you obtain:

- a good return with a low investment risk. Over a number of years, a well-chosen trust should produce a return on investment of over 12 per cent.

- hassle-free management. An investment trust saving scheme is designed for individual investors. It is easy to set up and maintain. The management of your investment is delegated to professionals, releasing you to get on with your life.

- no commissions and low fees. No commissions are necessary to set up a trust. Due largely to economies of scale, these trusts are the most cost-effective investment route for individual investors, with management fees of less than 1 per cent.

- a favourable tax treatment. Savings into an investment trust are not tax-deductible, but they do enjoy tax-free growth once in a trust. Income Tax and Capital Gains Tax can be levied when funds are withdrawn from a trust, although there are legal strategies that can be employed to minimize tax exposure.

- cost-effective investing. When you invest on a regular basis you are able to take advantage of a phenomenon known as *fixed cost averaging*. Investing regularly with a fixed sum automatically means you buy fewer shares at a premium and more shares when they are at a discount. The net effect is to reduce your average cost per share, which makes the 'drip-feed' approach far more cost effective than if you were purchasing a fixed number of shares, or making a lump sum purchase.

5 WHAT ABOUT TAX RELIEF?

WHAT TAX RELIEF SCHEMES?

'Wait a minute, Kate. There's something I don't understand here. These investment trusts sound ideal. We can obtain a good return on our savings, with little hassle and at minimal cost. I really like the fact that you can circumnavigate the financial advisors when setting one up, and that the regular monthly investing is going to benefit us in the long run. But I'm not convinced they're the best tax-free options available. You haven't even mentioned PEPs or ISAs, and these are specifically designed to provide individual investors with tax-free saving. Surely a tax-free scheme would be highly desirable for the Independence Fund?'

'Excuse me. What's a PEP?' asks Dan.

'Where have you been for the last decade?' I laugh.
He looks at me blankly. Kate comes to his rescue.

'Don't worry, Dan – you're not the only one. I only found out about them when I had to. PEP stands for Personal Equity Plan. It's effectively a Government plan to encourage individuals to save for their future. PEPs were introduced a few years ago and are to be replaced by the new Independent Savings Account, otherwise known as ISA. They're very similar schemes, although we know little about the ISA because the details have yet to be finalized.'

'So how do they help our Fund?'

'Well, the schemes reduce the tax you pay on your savings, although neither is an investment route per se. Both schemes are intended for use with an investment route of your choice, such as an investment trust. You can set up a PEP around most routes and then channel your savings through the scheme to avoid paying Income Tax and Capital Gains Tax.'

'Does this mean they are tax-deductible at source, like a pension plan?' he asks.

'You and your pension plans. No, they're not. You still have to pay tax on your earnings and save out of your net income. The tax relief comes into effect once you've put your savings into a scheme. You will not pay tax while in the scheme, nor when you withdraw your savings. This is the tax benefit of the scheme.'

'So this is definitely something we should set up for our Independence Fund, then?'

'Not necessarily.'

'Why not?'

'Well, there are a couple of catches.'

WHERE'S THE TAX BENEFIT?

The PEP was introduced to encourage people to save for their own future. The Government clearly encourages greater financial self-reliance, ultimately in the hope that this leads to less dependence on state benefits. Besides, it is also politically untenable to be levying Income Tax twice from an individual simply because he or she chooses to save money.

With a PEP or ISA you effectively avoid paying Income Tax and Capital Gains Tax on your savings. You are still obliged to pay tax at source, and this tax relief is effective only once your savings are in the scheme. Most importantly, there is no tax levied on any proceeds from a PEP. On the surface, this sounds great; no tax while in the scheme and no tax when you withdraw your savings. No wonder that so many people embrace PEPs without considering the real effect of the tax relief on their savings. Surprisingly, if you do not already have significant savings, the tax relief offered by a PEP will be negligible.

'I thought you said that we were aiming at a 13 per cent return over time?' Dan queries.

'We are. But remember the apple tree analogy – what produces your return on investment?'

'Well, the capital growth of your investment and your annual dividends. So your annual return is a combination of the two.'

'That's right. In a good trust the capital growth should produce, say, between 7 and 10 per cent, and the dividends, or return on income, will account for 2 to 3 per cent over the long term.'

'So the taxes are different too?'

'The Income Tax is levied on your dividends and the Capital Gains Tax is taxed on the annual capital growth in your Fund.'

INCOME TAX

Look at Income Tax first. With a PEP or ISA you'll avoid paying tax on your dividends, which is what Income Tax is levied on. The annual dividends in your Independence Fund will amount to about 2 to 3 per cent of your investment. By avoiding the tax on dividends, you are probably saving about half a per cent on your total savings each year – that is, 25 per cent of the 2 per cent dividend. If you have a large sum invested through a PEP, then of course this is going to be worthwhile. Half a per cent of £200,000 is £1,000 a year, which is certainly worthwhile. But if you're just starting an Independence Fund and you've decided to set up a PEP, a half per cent saving a year becomes slightly less impressive. A £1,000 investment put through a PEP could mean you've actually saved about only £5 in tax. This is almost certainly less than the charges you incur with the PEP, so you end up out of pocket.

CAPITAL GAINS TAX

Now consider Capital Gains Tax. This is a tax on the 'capital growth' of your savings. The capital growth is more significant than the dividend return. As ominous as it sounds, this tax only affects people who are drawing from very large funds. If you have just started your Independence Fund, then you are not going to pay Capital Gains Tax and the likelihood is that you will not even be liable to pay this tax for a good few years, until your Fund has grown substantially.

People are often confused over how Capital Gains Tax works. The tax is payable on the gain or profit realized when you sell your investment. The gain is calculated by the taxman. For example, imagine you sell shares for £30,000 from your Independence Fund to use as a downpayment on a house. Assume that these shares actually cost you £20,000 a few years ago. The taxman will let you compensate for inflation in the meantime and will allow you about £23,000 as your true cost. This produces a capital gain of £7,000; in other words, the proceeds of £30,000 less the calculated cost of £23,000. The taxman will look for tax on this £7,000 less your tax-free allowance for the year – which is £6,800 per person at present. You will therefore only have to pay tax on the difference, which at your current rate of taxation would be £200.

As you can see, funds can be drawn out without attracting much tax, especially if you are withdrawing funds over a few years. For instance, if you were cashing in £20,000 a year for three years to pay your way through university, the funds might well be tax-free. The Government raises very little from Capital Gains Tax and it's an easy tax to minimize.

SO WHAT?

The implications are clear. PEPs only really benefit investors who already have a large sum invested. The scheme is particularly useful for anyone who anticipates withdrawing large sums from their savings. In this situation, a PEP holder will be able to avoid paying significant taxes on his or her savings.

For investors with much smaller sums, the real impact of avoiding Income and Capital Gains Tax is minimal. For anyone starting an Independence Fund, the benefits are illusory; the tax savings are irrelevant and will remain so for many years. With such a marginal benefit, it is questionable whether you should opt for a PEP when starting your Independence Fund. As it happens, many investment trust savings schemes are now offering PEPs at no additional cost. If this is the case – and there isn't any additional charge for setting up or maintaining a PEP – then you might as well opt for it. You might as well have any tax relief available if it is offered at no charge.

COMMISSIONS AND CHARGES ON PEPS

Unfortunately, not all PEP schemes are so cost-effective. If you happen to have a PEP set up for you by an advisor, then you might be paying two sets of charges: his or her commission for setting it up, and the management fee of the underlying trust. The fee will vary, and as I've just mentioned some trusts offer PEPs at no additional charge to their usual annual management fee. If you're using an advisor, however, you will not avoid a commission – or sometimes a flat fee. Depending on your advisor and the underlying trust that has been chosen, you could actually be paying a combined advisor and management fee of 4 to 5 per cent on any savings you invest. There may be situations where you can justify paying these sorts of charges. But this will be unusual.

For the vast majority of investors – and certainly anyone starting a Fund – the charges on a PEP will outweigh any tax relief obtained, and so it is best to avoid them entirely for the moment. You can always consider tax relief schemes at a later date, when your exposure to tax is more significant. Unless you find a good investment trust that offers a PEP or ISA scheme at no extra cost, then you should just choose a good trust and worry about tax issues later.

Be aware also that three-quarters of a PEP has to be invested within the UK or the European Union. Only 25 per cent can be invested outside of these regions. Although there has been some relaxing of this restriction, it is another point you need to double check if you're looking at PEPs, bearing in mind your preference for a global trust for your Fund.

AFTER-THOUGHT

'What did you do about tax relief, Kate?' I ask.

'I didn't even consider PEPs when I started my Fund. The charges clearly outweighed the tax relief, so I didn't give them a second look. However, I'm sure there will come a time when the tax exposure on my Fund will justify investigating what tax-relief options are available. That's still a few years away, of course, and I'm hoping that the Government come up with a sensible and effective tax-relief scheme.'

'You'd think that the Government could support people who opt to set up their own Independence Fund,' I say. 'They've been making it easier to set up pensions for years now. Why not allow an individual to become increasingly self-reliant by extending tax relief to their Independence Fund? That would make a difference to the growth of the Fund, wouldn't it?'

'Provided there weren't all sorts of associated charges for a Government-registered scheme – which has always been the case to date,' Kate answers.

'Perhaps we need to write a letter to the PM outlining what we think is needed,' says Dan, enthused. 'I can dictate the

*letter now: Dear Prime Minister, do us all a favour and
ease up on taxes so that I can build up my own personal
Independence Fund and become financially self-sufficient. In
return, I'll be far less dependent on the Government for cash,
benefits, allowances and pensions. I'll also be far less tempted
to fiddle my income tax form. You know it makes sense.
Yours sincerely, Dan the man.'*

*'Not a bad idea, although I suspect we'll want to word it
differently.'*

SUMMARY

- The ideal environment is not necessarily that which appears
  to offer the highest tax relief. The tax benefits from a
  PEP are fairly irrelevant until you have a significant
  Independence Fund in place. The tax savings become
  worthwhile when your Fund nears £100,000. In the
  meantime, the tax savings are negligible.

- PEPs should only be considered where they are already
  offered on your chosen investment trust and involve no
  additional charge or restriction.

- Any charges over half of a per cent of the Fund will exceed
  the savings from tax-free dividends.

- ISAs are relatively new, but may well prove to be a suitable
  low-cost tax-free option for the Independence Fund.

6 WHAT ABOUT UNIT TRUSTS?

COMPARATIVE GROWTH

'Kate, you never did tell us about unit trusts,' I say.

'Thanks for reminding me. I've brought something along that will impress you.' She rummages through her bag and pulls out an issue of Investment Trust *magazine.*

'I came across a summary comparing the capital growth of an investment trust, unit trust, and building society account over the last 20 years. I'm using it for next week's article. The figures say it all. Here, have a look at it.'

AVERAGE GROWTH OF £1,000 INVESTED IN 1977 (INVESTOR EXPERIENCE)

	Investment Trust	Unit Trust	Building Society
1977	£1,000	£1,000	£1,000
1982	£2,186	£1,816	£1,566
1987	£10,391	£7,222	£2,354
1992	£11,552	£7,880	£3,667
1997	£20,115	£15,537	£4,596

'I'm not convinced,' I say after a while. 'You can prove anything with statistics these days, and everyone knows the share market has done very well over the last 20 years.'

'Of course it has. There's been unprecedented growth. That's not the issue. I'm concerned about the comparative performance of the three alternatives we have here: the investment trust, the unit trust, and the building society. Whatever the share market does overall, the respective performances are going to be similar to the pattern you see here. This demonstrates that, on average, investment trusts have outperformed average unit trusts at every stage in the last 20 years.'

'They did well against the building societies, too,' Dan says.

'Yes, but that goes without saying,' Kate replies.

'£20,000 instead of £4,600. That is some difference. Think of all those people who left their money in a building society account.' I suddenly remember that I have £1,000 in a building society account! I make a mental note to close it as soon as the Independence Fund is under way.

RELATIVE RETURNS

Calculating the average return on these three investment routes is enlightening, to say the least. It is difficult to replicate the accumulating effect unless you have access to a business calculator or spreadsheet software. The return on investment is shown here:

AVERAGE RETURN ON INVESTMENT FOR 1977–1997 (PERCENTAGE RETURN ON SAVINGS AT FIVE-YEAR INTERVALS)

	Investment Trust	Unit Trust	Building Society
1977	15.74%	11.99%	9.00%
1982	31.59%	27.93%	8.18%
1987	2.12%	1.75%	8.90%
1992	11.14%	13.66%	4.52%
1997	15.10%	13.79%	7.65%

The relative performances of the three investment routes clearly support the investment trust as the ideal choice. Remember that these are average returns – I do not want to give the impression that all investment trusts are better than all unit trusts. It's simply not the case, and you will definitely find some unit trusts outperforming some investment trusts on a regular basis. Another point to bear in mind is that although investment trusts have performed well on average, there will be a few that have done poorly. Not all investment trusts are close to this 15 per cent return on investment. I'd expect most to be above 10 per cent, and a good number huddled near the average, with a few trusts performing even better than this.

My chosen investment trust actually had a return of over 17 per cent for this same period of time. But there will also be trusts – perhaps specialist trusts – that under-perform. You cannot assume that all trusts will produce an equally good result. This is why you need to choose your optimal trust carefully.

THE DIFFERENCE WITH A UNIT TRUST

On the surface, unit and investment trusts appear similar. They're like cousins in a way; part of the 'trust' family, but somehow quite different. Financial advisors often gloss over the differences between a unit and investment trust.

An investment trust is a *closed* fund, which means that the total number of shares is determined when the trust is established. An investment trust has a fixed number of shares that can be bought and sold on the stockmarket. The managers of the fund may facilitate the buying and selling of shares, but their main responsibility is to make the right investment decisions and increase the value of the fund.

A unit trust is an *open* fund, which means that its size alters according to the number of shares purchased or sold. There is no fixed or upper limit of shares, and a unit trust's total value will rise and fall in line with the amount invested. This means that a unit trust is directly influenced by the shareholders' investment pattern. If an investor buys into a trust, the fund manager must make more investments. When shareholders want to sell their unit trust shares, the manager has to sell investments to pay them off. The problem is that this exposes the unit trusts to the whims of its shareholders, which can have a negative influence on the overall investment strategy of the trust. Investment decisions will be influenced by the changing demand for shares. An influx of cash might force fund managers to make investments at a bad time – for example just before a market slump. Equally, managers may have to sell shares to pay off shareholders at a time when they should be holding on to their investments. Unit trust managers are swayed by shareholder behaviour and this makes them more reactive to market changes. This may partly explain their slightly poorer average performance over the last 20 years.

THE COST OF A UNIT TRUST

Investing through a unit trust is usually more costly than investing through an investment trust. These higher fees associated with unit trusts might also be a reason why the average return to the investor from a unit trust is lower than its counterpart.

Charges within unit trusts vary. Initial charges are almost always higher than with investment trusts. Typical unit trusts charge between 3 and 5 per cent on entry. There will also be an annual management fee of between 1 and 2 per cent. In theory, you could be paying 7 per cent in the first year. Fees of this magnitude, which are at least double that of a typical investment trust, will seriously compromise the growth of your Fund. A shrewd investor would realize that to obtain a good return on his or her investment, a unit trust is going to have to perform that much better to compensate for these high charges. It is difficult for the unit trust management to make up for these charges through better performance.

Why does a unit trust cost so much more than an investment trust? Active marketing is the prime reason. The costs of advertising, producing brochures and paying commissions to intermediaries are high, and these are passed on to you, the investor, in the form of initial and ongoing fees. In contrast, the amount that an investment trust is allowed to spend on promotion and marketing is much more limited – that's why they are not so well known. The charges incurred buying and selling investments to cater to the shareholders' whims does not help keep costs down, either.

'Did you even consider a unit trust for your Independence Fund, Kate?'

'I did, but I was soon scared away by the comparatively high charges. If you're contemplating paying a 5 per cent commission, then that investment route has to perform that much better to compensate for the charge. I couldn't see any reason why the unit trust was going to perform any better than an investment trust I'd looked at. So I chose the investment trust, which had charges of 0.2 per cent. It was an easy decision, really.'

Dan leans back in his chair. 'I wish I'd known all this last month,' he says. 'I spoke to this financial advisor who was recommending a unit trust PEP. I remember his commissions seemed fairly reasonable at the time. Of course, I knew nothing about unit trusts and PEPs. That's the problem, isn't it? If you don't know what questions to ask, then you can't challenge an advisor.'

'Did you sign up to the plan in the end?'

'Oh, no. I didn't have any money anyway.'

THE LIFE INSURANCE OPTION

'The same advisor also recommended that I take out a life insurance plan.'

'But why did he say that? You don't have any dependants.'

'I know. But he was offering a saving scheme and insurance plan all in one. It sounded like a two-in-one deal.'

'You mean a life insurance endowment plan?'

'That's the one. What do you think of it?'

LIFE INSURANCE ENDOWMENT PLAN

A life insurance endowment plan is not a viable option for your Fund. Avoid one at all cost. This is how it works: You agree the amount you want to be insured for, and then set up a savings scheme where you invest money on a regular basis until you reach that sum. If you don't happen to die, you'll be able to collect the amount that your endowment plan has generated. If you do happen to die, your dependants will receive your savings and the balance of the sum insured, provided by the insurance company.

The problem with these plans is that they are a compromise between a life insurance plan and a savings scheme. In almost all situations, it would be simpler and more cost-effective to keep these elements entirely separate. For a start, you do not need life insurance if you have no dependants. If you *have* got dependants, then you'd be far better off purchasing 'term insurance' that can be tailored to your requirements – covering a child, for instance, until he or she attains the age of 21.

The savings part of an endowment plan is often an equally poor deal. An endowment plan requires you to make regular monthly payments into a fund that is usually linked to fixed-interest Government bonds or gilts. Although these are very secure investments, they are likely only to produce 6 to 7 per cent interest on your savings. As we already know, you can do better than this.

'Just as well I didn't sign anything. It almost calls for a quiet celebration down at the pub. What do you say?'

'Not a bad idea. The sun has come out. We could even sit outside.'

SUMMARY

On average, investment trusts perform significantly better than unit trusts. A good example is to consider performance over the last 20 years, where:

- £1,000 invested in 1977 in an average investment trust will have produced £20,115, representing a 15 per cent return on savings.

- The same £1,000 invested in an average unit trust would have produced £15,537, representing a 13 per cent return on savings.

- In the same 20-year period, a building society savings account would have produced £4,596, representing a 7½ per cent return on savings.

Heavy marketing expenditure often hampers the performance of unit trusts, and although investment trusts do not have as slick an image, they do perform.

A life insurance endowment plan and other 'two-in-one combinations' are poor alternatives for the Independence Fund, and should be avoided.

7 WHAT ABOUT PENSION PLANS?

OUT FOR A DRINK

Kate insists on buying the drinks in return for lunch. She goes inside to fetch them, while we take up a table outside in the sun.

'What a waste of time leaving that £1,000 of mine in a building society account,' I say despondently to Dan.

'It could have been worse, though. Imagine if you'd found out 20 years from now?' Dan responds.

'That's true. Finding out that you could have had £20,000 instead of just over £4,500 would have been a bit harsh.

Mind you, if we hadn't met Kate, we'd have our savings in a "Super Saver" building society account earning next to nothing. Where would that have got us?'

'Probably to Majorca and back for a couple of weeks. Kate told me on the way down that her investment trust produced an even higher return.'

'By how much?'

'Seventeen per cent annual return. By the time she's had it for 20 years, her investment trust could produce £30,000 from an original investment of £1,000.' I'm stunned. We watch silently as Kate negotiates the door with three pints in hand.

'What's up? You two look a bit lost. Have I been that boring?' she asks, settling the drinks on the table.

'Just thinking about returns on investment,' says Dan absent-mindedly.

'With an investment trust, that is,' I add.

'You realize that when you start your Independence Fund, you'll be investing more than the £1,000 I did at first, so the result will be cumulative. Fixed cost averaging makes a difference too, so you'll end up with a substantial sum after 20 years.'

'Why don't we just put our savings into your investment trust, Kate?'

'Definitely not, choose your own,' she says, taking a sip of beer. 'Now, let's move on to what other alternatives you might consider for your Independence Fund. So far we've looked at investment trusts, unit trusts, a bank account and life insurance endowment policies. What else is there?'

'You mentioned pension plans a few times,' I say. 'But if we've set up an Independence Fund, do we really need a pension plan as well?'

DIFFERENT ROLES

Don't expect your Independence Fund to do two jobs at the same time. The Fund is designed to produce an essential income within your working life and for your working life. It is unrealistic to assume that it will also provide a substantial retirement income as well.

For a start, it is possible that you might use the Fund long before you even retire. There might be an entirely unforeseen event that forces you to draw out your independence savings; you could be made redundant when you're 45, or you might decide to make a career change, which will jeopardize the chance of using these independence savings in retirement. You must secure and guarantee a minimum retirement income and not merely hope that the Independence Fund might provide for retirement as well as your working life. In other words, you need a pension plan as well as an Independence Fund. Don't despair, though – this does not mean the end of your disposable income. The aim is to produce a basic retirement income, not to create a plan to rival the Independence Fund.

THE ADVANTAGES

Fortunately there are some attractions to taking out a pension plan.

GROSS CONTRIBUTIONS

For one thing, you do not pay income tax on contributions into a pension plan. Instead of paying income tax on your earnings –

usually at 25 per cent – the Government allows you to invest this amount with your net contribution into your own pension plan. So instead of paying tax you make 'gross' contributions into your own plan. The savings are significant: for every 75 pence you contribute, the tax relief is worth an additional 25 pence. In other words, for every pound you invest into a pension plan, the Government will contribute 33 pence. If you happen to pay tax at the higher tax bracket of 40 per cent, then the tax relief amounts to 40 pence for every 60 pence you invest. Put another way, for every pound you invest, the Government will contribute 66 pence. The tax relief on a pension plan is significant for two reasons: it accelerates the growth of your pension fund and you can use less of your own savings to generate a reasonable pension fund.

NO TAX ON INCOME OR CAPITAL GAINS

There is no tax on income or capital gains while your savings are in a pension fund. This allows your tax-free savings to accumulate all the while they are invested.

YOUR EMPLOYER MAKES AN OFFER YOU CANNOT REFUSE

In some instances, your employer may offer you a non-contributory pension. This means the company makes payments on your behalf at no cost to you. Clearly, this is always going to be worthwhile. Some company schemes will match your contributions pound for pound, which is an equally attractive option. Be cautious of arrangements where your company only offers to cover the cost of administering the plan. These are not necessarily good deals, and you'll need to have a close look before committing.

These are the three main benefits of a plan. At first glance, a pension plan seems an ideal way to save, thanks primarily to the tax relief offered on the contributions. But there are some drawbacks.

THE DRAWBACKS

A pension plan is a Government-approved scheme intended to encourage an individual to save for retirement. Since the Government is offering significant tax relief, it needs to ensure that pension plans are administered properly and that pension funds can only be used towards an individual's retirement. This results in a heavily administered scheme with some prominent disadvantages.

HIGH ADMINISTRATIVE COSTS

The Government has set up rules and regulations to prevent abuse of the pension plan. Pension advisors claim that administering pension plans is time-consuming and requires considerable paperwork. They have to charge for this, and the costs of running a plan are deducted directly from your pension contributions. The charges will vary and can be exceptionally high. In some cases, total administrative charges have amounted to as much as 25 per cent of your savings, which will wipe out much of the tax-free benefit you gain from a plan. In particular, front-loaded charges are notoriously damaging to the long-term growth of your plan.

NO ACCESS TO YOUR MONEY

Savings in a pension plan are locked away and you cannot touch these funds until you've retired. You cannot borrow against your pension plan or use it in the meantime. To make matters worse, if you are not happy with the performance of your pension fund, transferring to another investment company is a complicated and expensive process. Transfer charges and other penalties are solely intended to discourage individuals from switching pension companies.

TAXABLE PROCEEDS

Although there is no tax on your savings while invested in a pension fund, the proceeds of a plan are subject to income tax. In other words, you will be liable to pay tax on the proceeds of your plan, just as if you were earning a salary.

RESTRICTED USE OF FUNDS

When you retire and 'cash in' your plan, at least 75 per cent of your funds *must* be used to purchase an annuity, which is a guaranteed income for life. Usually the annuity is bought from the same life insurance company that handled your pension fund, although in practice you are able to choose an annuity from another company. The remaining 25 per cent of your pension fund on retirement is tax-free and can be taken as cash.

Don't forget that when you do eventually buy an annuity, the insurance company takes the whole capital sum. In addition, if you purchase an annuity early, your annual income will be considerably reduced, as the pension company will have to pay out for longer.

'What is an annuity?'

'For a lump sum you purchase an annuity to provide an income for the rest of your life. The company paying the annuity calculates statistically your average life expectancy and pays you an income. This is in effect part return of your

capital and part interest on the remaining balance for as long as you live. They have to make cautious assumptions, as people are living longer and they cannot take too much of a risk with their investments. Recently, one life insurance company was criticized for effectively paying interest at 4½ per cent on their annuities over a 30- to 40-year period. Compare that to a good investment trust, which would have been growing at 13 per cent.'

SO WHAT'S THE PLAN?

You are probably wondering whether it is worth putting money into a pension plan at all, given these drawbacks. The fact is if you don't, no one else will. The Government has been progressively reducing the State pension that will be available in retirement, alarmed no doubt by the escalating cost of Social Security benefits. The current basic pension is only £60 per week for a single person, and £100 per week for a married couple. This only represents about 25 per cent of the income of the average 'breadwinner', in other words the main income earner in a household. This is barely enough to exist on. The percentage is likely to decline steadily as the Government off-loads the responsibility for a pension onto the individual, although earnings-related supplements will improve pension income. The message is that the Government expects you to provide for your own retirement.

So how much should you reasonably put aside for your later years, when you're no longer earning? If you listen to pension advisors, it is impossible to put too much aside. They'll recommend you build as large a pension fund as possible to ensure a reasonable lifestyle once you've retired. They'll warn against the ravages of inflation, changes in Government regulations, the possibility that your pension fund does not perform well, and that people always spend far more in retirement than expected. They usually also add that you have left it rather late to start your plan, and should really try to catch up by making some 'healthy' monthly contributions now. Too often pension advisors generate such mystique and hype that it is difficult to know what to do. There is a route through the maze, however.

THE PLAN

The solution is to set up a pension plan that will provide you with a minimum reasonable income in retirement. You can decide at a later date whether you wish to contribute more into your plan. This will depend on your personal financial situation – and the status of your Independence Fund will no doubt feature highly in your decision. In the meantime, you can take comfort from the fact that you have initiated a basic plan and have secured a minimum income for when you retire. There are three main steps to achieving this.

STEP ONE

Make one payment of between £300 and £500 a year into a personal pension plan.

Although income from a pension plan is fully taxable, personal exemptions allow you to receive up to £8,000 a year tax-free. Any tax-deductible contributions that result in tax-free retirement income will be worthwhile. Once your retirement income exceeds your allowances, you begin to pay tax.

If you want the most tax-efficient pension plan, then your objective must be to ensure that when you make tax-deductible contributions the eventual pension received is tax-free. One way to do this is to create a pension plan that will produce a pension income equal to your tax-free allowance. For example, saving £300 a year before tax for 30 years at a 10 per cent growth rate will create a pension fund of about £50,000. Assuming a 10 per cent annual return, this will produce a retirement income of about £5,000 per annum. Combined with your State pension, which is worth about £3,000 a year, you will have secured a retirement income of £8,000, which coincides with your tax-free allowance. Any further contributions above this allowance will be subject to income tax at 25 per cent or more.

STEP TWO

Make contributions to your pension plan to avoid paying tax at higher rates.

If your income attracts tax at a higher rate, say 40 per cent, then channel the excess into your pension plan. Until your retirement income exceeds twice the average breadwinner income – which is about £40,000 in today's value, you will be paying tax at about 25 per cent. Therefore, if you can achieve tax relief on additional savings of more than 25 per cent, you are probably going to achieve the second objective.

'Do you have any trouble keeping up your pension contributions on your freelance salary, Kate?'

'Not really. Although my income varies wildly at times, I am always able to contribute something towards a basic pension every year. Now I've started to do well and my annual earnings have improved. In the last year or so, some of my savings have been liable to the 40 per cent tax. I decided to put this amount straight into my pension plan.'

'So the 40 per cent tax went towards your pension instead?'

'That's right. It's the same as the Government contributing 40 pence to every 60 pence you pay. It makes a plan very worthwhile, especially if you're only going to be taxed at 25 per cent when you withdraw your pension savings. I've worked out that if I have one year in four where I can contribute £2,500 into my plan with a 40 per cent tax saving, then I should easily reach my minimum retirement income target of £20,000 a year.'

'That's all very well, but I'm not likely to be earning that much in the coming years. What are my options if I'm not going to be paying tax at 40 per cent? Do I just stick with the minimum pension plan?'

'Clearly, £8,000 per annum is not much to live on when you retire. Remember that this is a minimum amount only; if you want a reasonable income in retirement you'll need to bolster your pension fund somehow. One option is to rely on the Independence Fund, but the dangers of over-dependence have already been mentioned: you might use your savings before you retire, leaving you with little to exist on. The alternative is to increase your pension contributions and accept that your pension savings are irretrievable until you retire.'

A compromise is inevitable. There is no magic formula to follow. Remember that you have about 30 years to contribute enough for a basic pension of £20,000 per annum, which works out to be about £600 or £700 a year. The final decision on the size of pension plan you want and how you generate that amount depends largely on your own financial situation. Invariably this will be influenced by how well your Independence Fund is doing and whether you're prepared to lock away funds now for your pension, or keep your options open and transfer savings from your Fund into a pension scheme at a later date. Perhaps the best-fit solution is to aim for a reasonable pension that will produce at least £20,000 per annum, and keep the rest of your savings in the Independence Fund. Although you do want a guaranteed income in retirement, you should retain the initiative on the rest of your savings.

STEP THREE

Contract out of the State Earnings Related Pension Scheme (SERPS).

If you are employed, your employer has to make contributions on your behalf into the State scheme. You should ask your employer to help you contract out of the State scheme. As a result, part of your employer's contributions will now be paid directly into your own pension plan. This step will not cost you a penny, but will improve your pension income in retirement.

ASSUMPTIONS MADE

This plan of action is based on current facts and assumptions. It is assumed that these relationships will remain proportionally the same over the years to come, although the actual values will rise steadily in line with inflation and average earnings. The assumptions are that:

- The average 'breadwinner' income is currently £20,000 a year before tax.

- At present, a couple enjoys tax-free allowances of £8,000 a year, or say about 40 per cent of the average income. Earnings over this amount are subject to a tax of about 25 per cent.

- You are exposed to higher rates of tax once you start to earn over about £40,000 of income. The higher tax bracket is expected to remain at twice the average income.

- The primary aim is to achieve a minimum retirement income of £20,000 every year, on the basis of current values and salaries. The state pension will probably provide a single person with £3,000 of this amount, leaving a shortfall of £17,000 to be covered by a personal pension plan. Assuming a 10 per cent rate of return on your annuity or investment is possible, you will need to generate £170,000 to meet this shortfall, which is the gap between the State pension and your target amount, which is the average 'breadwinner' income.

A FEW GOLDEN RULES

- Pick a good pension plan. Be aware that the performance of different pension plans varies widely; you will need to pick one as carefully as you've chosen an investment trust. Expert advice is essential in order to choose a good plan, although you do not need to pay extortionate commissions to obtain it. Pay a pension advisor a fee for advice rather than allowing him or her to charge a commission on your plan. This will work out to be much cheaper in the long run.

- Make single annual premium payments into your pension plan. It is better to make a lump sum payment at the end of the year if you can, when you know your total income for the year. By doing this, you will save on commissions and administrative charges.

- Switch companies if your plan is performing badly. If your pension fund is not performing well, you might be dissuaded to transfer your savings to another company by high 'transfer penalties'. If this is the case, simply halt that plan and place all future savings with a different company.

This is the minimum pension provision you should make. As mentioned, larger plans will have to be at your discretion and dependent on your personal financial circumstances. Speak to a good independent financial advisor for specific advice on your own situation.

By the way, do not expect many advisors to agree with these assumptions, or the plan of action for that matter. Pension plans are probably the most lucrative of financial schemes, so an advisor is not going to discourage you from contributing all you possibly can into your pension plan. Just don't forget who pays the commission or charges you see in a plan.

MOVING ON

'It's like asking turkeys to vote for an early Christmas,'
Dan says, finally.

'What is?'

'Asking pension advisors to agree with Kate's scheme.'

'That's one way of expressing it, I suppose,' she says, looking at her watch. 'This pub must have extended hours; I didn't realize it was so late. I'm going to have to leave you.'

Dan drains his pint. 'We can't tempt you with another half, then?'

'No, thanks. I'm doing some painting this afternoon. Are you clear about how to manage a pension plan now?'

'I think so. We set up a basic pension plan to ensure a minimum income for when we retire. We make one-off payments each year to avoid excess charges, and aim to put away an amount that will generate at least an average income in retirement – or more if we can afford to.'

'And?'

'What else? If we're taxed at 40 per cent then it's really worth contributing to obtain tax relief at 40 per cent. We should also opt out of the State scheme and consider any company schemes on offer. Just my luck that my company doesn't have any scheme at all. Finally, we need to choose a good pension plan carefully.'

'Imagine earning enough to pay tax at 40 per cent. What a concept,' Dan says, leaning back in his chair. Kate moves to get up.

'Kate,' I say, not wanting her to leave us in limbo. 'I'm clear about what to do about our pension plan and how we combine it with our Independence Fund. But what about when we decide to buy a home? Isn't there a conflict of interest there too?' Kate sighs and slumps back into her chair.

'What are you up to tomorrow?' she asks. We both shrug.

'It's a Bank Holiday.'

'I know. Come over to my place after lunch – and bring some overalls.'

SUMMARY

The Independence Fund is *not* an alternative to a pension plan. It is designed to provide essential financial support throughout life, although in some cases it could also provide a supplementary income in retirement.

A basic pension plan is recommended in order to secure a reasonable income in retirement. The main advantages of a pension plan are that:

- contributions into a plan are tax free
- there is no Income or Capital Gains Tax on your pension fund
- a pension annuity is guaranteed for the rest of your life.

A large pension plan is not necessarily advisable, as the benefits of a plan may be significantly reduced by:

- high commissions and administrative costs
- low investment performance
- restrictions on the use of the pension fund at retirement
- the risk that annuity interest rates and resulting pensions are low at retirement
- taxation.

Kate's method maximizes the likelihood that the funds put into a pension plan will achieve an acceptable return on investment and result in a basic minimum pension of £20,000 a year at today's values.

Contributions into a pension plan and the Independence Fund will ultimately need to be set according to your individual financial priorities.

8 AND PROPERTY?

'You could have told us the walls were 10-foot high. How are we going to reach up there with a paintbrush?' Dan says, pointing at the ceiling. We're both standing in Kate's main room, barefoot and in some old clothes.

'I've a step ladder in the kitchen,' she answers confidently. Not that we think it'll make much of a difference. We spend some time working out our painting strategy, which amounts to each taking a corner of the room, washing down the walls and applying copious amounts of sunflower emulsion. Paintbrushes are soon dipping and swishing.

'Wait till we tell Bob that Kate had us paying for her financial services in hard labour,' Dan says.

'Just make sure he realizes you mean painting and decorating,' she says, eyebrows raised. *'What do you think of the flat, by the way?'*

'Very spacious. I like the fact that it's on the ground floor and fairly open-plan. Ideal really. When can we move in?'

'When you agree to do all the cooking and cleaning.'

'You're safe there, Kate. He'll never agree to that,' I say. *'It's a beautiful flat. So you bought it recently?'*

'As soon as I knew I would be in London for at least two years. As it happens it worked out very well. I was able to use my Independence Fund for the downpayment.'

'Really? I thought you said we shouldn't raid the Fund for a few years.'

'Unless there is a justifiable need – and buying a home is certainly one of them. Besides, making use of the Fund for a home purchase is not a waste. A home is an investment in itself. You've just altered the state of your investment, that's all.'

'It makes me wonder why Dan and I bother renting sometimes. I've always shied away from buying a place. Do you think we're wasting our money renting?'

'No. It really depends on your personal circumstances. Renting is far more flexible, although buying your own place can be more worthwhile in the long term.'

'But is it possible to buy a home and still have an Independence Fund? Surely the two are in conflict for your savings?'

'Not necessarily.'

ACCOMMODATION AND THE FUND

Unless you have access to free accommodation, you will have to either rent or buy a place to live. It won't take you long to notice that the UK property market favours home ownership rather than renting. Compared to continental Europe and North America, people in the UK tend to own rather than rent their homes.

The drawback of this is that finding rented property is often time-consuming. You'll know about this if you've spent any time trying to secure a place through *LOOT*, the *Evening Standard* or any local property paper. There's a very high demand and you pay a high price for your accommodation. Renting is prohibitively expensive, the quality available is often poor, and there's a lack of choice. It is wise to rent when you are seeking a flexible arrangement, but if you're settling for longer than about two years, it is probably worthwhile to buy somewhere. In contrast to renting, there is a much greater choice for the homebuyer, and despite the property slump of the early 1990s and the emergence of negative equity, buying is still the best option for the long term.

BUYING A HOME

Ultimately, a home is somewhere to live and the overriding condition is that you are comfortable living there in the first place. As you're no doubt aware, a home is also an investment. It's as much an investment as buying stocks and shares, or investing in a trust for that matter. Provided a home is chosen carefully, it can be a sound and stable investment over the long term.

Choosing a good property is critical. Estate agents may claim that location is paramount, but you also need to consider the property's condition, cost of maintenance, and the immediate neighbourhood. The timing of a property purchase and the subsequent time of sale are equally important. But this is the sort of thing that you'll have heard many people droning on and on about.

> 'There's often a lot of pressure to buy a home. My parents were obsessed about me having my own place to live in. Maybe they wanted to make sure that I wouldn't end up back with them once I'd left. Whatever the motive, having a foot on the "first rung of the housing ladder" was all that concerned them. It was the best investment they'd ever made; therefore it had to be the best investment I could make. The fact was, it was the only investment they actually ever did make, apart from a few British Gas shares. So they didn't really have anything to compare it with.'

> 'But it's meant to be an excellent hedge against inflation.'

> 'A hedge against inflation, security for life, pride in owning your home, home improvements increase its value, blah, blah, blah. It sounds as if we have like-minded parents. Perhaps we can put them together in a room and start a mutual appreciation society.'

> 'But are they right?'

BENEFITS OF A HOME PURCHASE

A home is a sound and stable investment for most homeowners. The long-term value is still likely to rise steadily, at between 8 and 10 per cent per annum. Although the return on property may not be as impressive as a good investment trust, it does hold its value against inflation. A home is not only a sound investment, it also offers some other unique advantages:

- You can borrow up to 95 per cent of the cost. In other words, you can obtain a property worth more than 10 times as much as your downpayment.
- You can borrow at an advantageous interest rate by taking out a mortgage.
- The interest due on the borrowed amount is tax-deductible, although the Government now restricts this to 10 per cent relief on the first £30,000 borrowed.
- There is a wide selection of properties to choose from.
- You can increase the value of your investment by making home improvements.
- You may be able to use the property to negotiate a loan, as the value of your investment improves over time.
- There are no Capital Gains Taxes when you come to sell your house.

Owning a home is certainly a worthwhile investment, provided the individual circumstances are right. However, as a home will require a substantial financial commitment, the question arises as to whether the Independence Fund can be sustained alongside a home purchase? A few years ago, the answer may well have been 'no'. It used to be difficult to borrow on a mortgage and choices were restrictive. In fact, you only had one real option; the standard 'repayment mortgage'.

THE REPAYMENT MORTGAGE

Building societies used to offer only a repayment mortgage. With this mortgage, your monthly payments would cover the interest on the borrowing, the essential insurance to cover the lender, and the repayment of a bit of the original amount borrowed – the capital. In time, your monthly payments went increasingly towards repaying the capital. Repayment mortgages were relatively costly.

THE ENDOWMENT-LINKED MORTGAGE

A refinement of the traditional repayment mortgage was the 'endowment-linked' mortgage, where monthly payments were used to pay just the interest on the loan, and a savings plan was set up to pay off the amount borrowed over perhaps 25 or 30 years.

One advantage of this was that you could then claim tax relief on the whole of the interest every month rather than see this as a declining benefit. In addition, provided your funds were well invested in a good endowment plan, which was usually linked to a mix of bonds and shares, then the endowment plan would provide some capital growth. This meant you could reduce monthly payments slightly in anticipation of this capital growth. The endowment mortgage could provide a lower total monthly cost to the homeowner and was considered an improvement on the standard repayment mortgage. However, it would still be difficult to transfer your investment or endowment plan from one company to another without paying penalties or other charges imposed by the lender.

THE MORTGAGE OPTIONS TODAY

There is now much more competition for your borrowings, and mortgage arrangements are far more flexible. You can make 'interest-only' monthly payments to a bank or building society at a comparatively low rate. You can avoid combined life insurance packages and take out term insurance, which is far more economic. Most importantly, you can create an investment plan to pay off the original sum far more effectively than you could in the past. Not only do you have a greater selection of investments for your plan, but also you can switch investment funds in search of a better long-term return.

One popular option at present is to use your pension fund to pay off the capital, instead of choosing a separate plan. This is not always the wisest of options, however. Only 25 per cent of the final sum accumulated can be used to pay off the mortgage on your house, as the remaining 75 per cent must be used to purchase an annuity on retirement. Although you will enjoy tax relief on your pension contributions, this restriction means you will need to save considerably more to pay off the house loan. This could result in a higher monthly payment. You might also find yourself contractually tied in and paying substantial commissions up front!

There is an alternative, however. Your Independence Fund can be used to pay off a mortgage. This may mean increasing the amount of money you put aside every month to cover both the mortgage and your 'independence' requirements, but the benefits of a well-chosen investment trust might well make this worthwhile.

KEY POINTS

Whichever arrangement you choose, make sure that you can keep up the monthly payments. As a rule, the interest payments should not exceed what you would pay in rent for the equivalent accommodation. In addition, there are a number of other essential points to bear in mind when arranging a mortgage.

Don't Pay Off the Principal Early

Providing your Independence Fund is performing satisfactorily, resist the temptation to pay off principal from the mortgage early. For example, if the mortgage interest rate is at 7 per cent (net) and your Fund is growing at 15 per cent per annum, it does not make sense to use your independence savings to pay off the mortgage. All you are doing is simply increasing your monthly payment and depriving yourself of 15 per cent growth on these savings. Think of the interest payments every month as 'rent'.

Make Sure that You Can Afford the Mortgage and the Independence Fund

Choose a property within the reach of your downpayment and income. Ensure monthly interest payments and the monthly savings paid into your Independence Fund are reasonable given your earnings. Remember that there are other charges that need to be paid: council tax, lighting, heating, water and so on. You will also have to purchase term insurance to protect against premature death, or perhaps other eventualities such as redundancy and sickness. If this is all looking costly, consider renting out one of the rooms in your house to help the cash flow.

Property Investments Will Rise and Fall

Although property has steadily risen over many years, it can go down as well, just like stocks and shares. This is why you need to consider it a long-term investment.

Choose a Good Investment

Finally, make sure your home is a good investment for you: pay a reasonable price, choose a property that will be easy to sell on, and choose something appropriate for your budget. The costs of purchasing or selling a home, and the work involved, do not make buying a home an ideal short-term investment.

Maintenance

A home requires far more work than an investment trust. It is important to keep the property in good condition, which means either doing the decorating and repair work yourself, or paying someone else to do it for you.

Good Neighbourhood

It is key to have property in a suburb that is stable or improving rather than one that might be deteriorating.

Mortgage Protection Insurance

You may be required by a lender to purchase mortgage protection insurance, which serves to protect the lender's interests, not yours. It should be avoided wherever possible, as it is usually very expensive. Increasing your downpayment slightly might mean you do not have to pay it at all.

DOWNPAYMENT

In addition to paying off the mortgage, the Independence Fund could be used for a downpayment on a home. Draw out the minimum amount required for the downpayment, typically 5 to 10 per cent. You can legitimately regard this as an investment, and moreover one where you are entitled to the entire rise in value of the property. Leverage or gearing is a distinct advantage of a property purchase; with a downpayment of 10 per cent you can benefit from owning an asset worth 10 times that amount.

'I set up my Fund six years ago and have paid in about £170 per month since then. By the time I came to buy a home, the Fund was worth £20,000.'

'Some apple tree,' Dan whistles. 'How much did you take out for the downpayment?'

'£8,000. This place was worth about £80–90,000, so I took out £8,000, which left me with £12,000 in my Fund. It didn't worry me at all. I knew I'd made a good choice and the property would retain its value. I just considered the downpayment as an investment – almost an extension of the Fund, if you like.'

MOVING ON

'So we can use the Fund for a downpayment and for paying off the mortgage as well?'

'That's right.'

'Except we couldn't do that until we had built up our Fund for a few years.'

'True, but even if you couldn't use your Fund for the downpayment, you could use it eventually to repay your mortgage. These are just ideas based on what I'm doing. You need to bear them in mind, and then when you do come to buy a home look at all your options – including using the Fund as I've just mentioned.'

'Even so, Kate, you've just reminded me of all the advantages of having your own place. I know I'm going to be in London for at least a couple of years. I think I'll buy a place. I could always rent out a room to Dan.'

'Have you as a landlord?' Dan exclaims. 'Unlikely – you're bad enough as a flatmate!'

'I'll remind you of that when you come begging for a room.'

'I think it's time for a tea break,' Kate announces. 'I'll make the tea, if you two can clear up the mess.'

'You mean clear up your mess, Kate,' I say, indicating the shambles where she's been painting. She gets up from the stool and walks sharply out of the room. For a moment we think she's offended, but she returns straightaway with two typed A4 sheets of paper.

'This is "Kate's Starter Kit",' she says, handing us each a copy. 'I decided to write a short guide on how to set up the Independence Fund. You might as well have a copy now, seeing that you were droning on about it earlier. It shows you how to select an ideal investment trust for your savings.'

'So you want us to work through this now?' I ask.

'Do it in your own time. It shouldn't take you long.'

'That's what the teachers at school used to say, and it would take ages,' Dan moans.

'You know most of this already because we've spent the entire weekend talking about it. Look on the bright side; by the time you finish this guide, you'll have chosen an excellent investment trust and started your Independence Fund. We should perhaps arrange to meet up after you've made your selection. There are still two aspects I need to talk through.'

'What are they?'

'How to sustain and use the Fund in the long term.'

'But I thought we could forget about it once we set it up?'
I protest.

'You do forget about it. But there is a minimum maintenance required once a year to check that your chosen trust is doing well. There are also a few techniques you should know about which will ensure you can use the Fund without harming its long-term growth.'

'Sounds good to me,' Dan nods appreciatively.

'Now let's make some tea. Can you make it, Dan? I wouldn't want my kettle to end up sunflower yellow.'

SUMMARY

You can build an Independence Fund and buy your own home at the same time. Remember that:

- The Independence Fund can provide for your downpayment or deposit.

- *The monthly interest payments should be regarded as rent.*

- Payments into your Independence Fund need to be increased since the Fund will eventually be used to pay off the mortgage.

- Property is still likely to be a good investment over the longer term, and one which is tax free when you sell.

9 KATE'S 'STARTER KIT'

HOW TO SELECT AN INVESTMENT TRUST FOR YOUR INDEPENDENCE FUND

1. WHAT YOU NEED

- three hours to yourself
- a recent edition of the AITC *Monthly Information Service* (*see below*)
- a pen
- a notepad
- a ruler
- (optional): a cup of coffee and light music in the background.

2. WHAT YOU DO

Step One: Gather the Essential Information
Order a copy of the AITC *Monthly Information Service*.

The *Monthly Information Service*, produced by the Association of Investment Trust Companies, or AITC for short, is essential to your selection of an investment trust. It is a monthly magazine that records and compares the performance of all investment trusts in the UK. It is normally available on subscription only, although the AITC do send out one sample to those who request it.

To order a copy, call the AITC on 0171-282 5555 and ask them for their most recent monthly issue. Invariably, you'll be asked if you've ever received one in the past, to which you'll honestly answer 'no'. Someone will then take your details and post the magazine to you. As the periodical is sold on subscription, do not expect the AITC to send repeat issues at no cost. Whether you wish to subscribe or not is entirely up to you. For the purposes of choosing an investment trust, you only need the one issue.

Don't panic when the periodical arrives through your letterbox. It can be rather intimidating when you first start to leaf through it – but it's no more complicated than a supermarket till receipt. There are also explanatory notes at the back that might be helpful.

The AITC magazine is all you need to choose a good investment trust for your Independence Fund, although I'm sure that if you told this to a financial advisor, he or she would produce a dozen arguments to the contrary. It provides virtually all the impartial information you will need to make an informed decision on a suitable trust for your Independence Fund.

Before selecting the investment trust, familiarize yourself with the AITC publication. Designed for financial advisors and private investors, this unique magazine contains information on the 300-odd UK investment trusts. It produces comparative reports on the performance of each trust, and lists their respective total assets, the worldwide spread of investments, and details on savings schemes and charges. It also identifies which investment company manages which trust.

The Performance Comparison on the first page is certainly worth glancing at. It shows how investment trusts have fared against unit trusts, the retail prices index, the FTSE indexes and a high-interest 30-day bank account (for anyone who happens to have £50,000 to spare). The returns are shown for a theoretical £100 investment after a 1-, 3-, 5- and 10-year period.

Have a look at how investment trusts are doing compared to the FTSE Actuaries All Share Index.

You may find that the average investment trusts don't perform better than the FTSE. If that is the case, you might want to consider taking out a 'tracker fund', which is a trust that mirrors the performance of the FTSE Index (see page 39). Before jumping to the conclusion that this is the easiest option, bear in mind that the performance figures shown are averages, and if you follow this guide through you will choose an investment trust that is performing well above both the average and the FTSE Index.

As an investor, you need to know how your trust is performing. The acid test for performance is the return on your original investment, which is expressed in two ways: as the 'return on share price', and as the 'net asset value'. The share price return indicates the market value of the shares. This is usually below its real value, otherwise known as the 'net asset value' or NAV. The NAV is the true value of the underlying assets. If a trust was to be closed and all the shareholders paid off, their return would be based on the net asset value of the trust. Just think of the share price as what the 'market will pay' and the NAV as the 'sum of the values' of the underlying investments.

Share Price Total Return on £100

	1yr	3yr	5yr	10yr
An Investment Trust	£135.80	£192.90	£214.10	£466.30
Size-weighted Average	£124.40	£171.70	£198.70	£430.90

The return on investment is always expressed in terms of what you would receive now if you had invested £100 1 year ago, 3 years ago, 5 years ago or 10 years ago. For example, imagine you had invested £100 five years ago in the above trust – it would be now worth £214.10. Equally, £100 invested 10 years ago in this trust would have accumulated into £466.30 at current market prices.

For Further Information

If you'd like further information, then read a magazine called *Investment Trusts* which, as its name suggests, is dedicated to the world of investment trusts in the UK. It tends to have fairly accessible articles aimed at the private investor.

There is also an American magazine called *Forbes*. The August edition gives a challenging but comprehensive insight into Mutual Funds, the American equivalent to investment trusts. Mutual Funds are far more developed in the United States, with approximately 10 times as many trusts to choose from.

CHOOSING THE IDEAL TRUST

Step Two: Choose an International Trust

Back to your AITC *Monthly Information Service*. A glance at the Performance Comparison at the beginning of the document will list the various types of investment trusts available, such as: UK General, North America, Far East, Property, or Emerging Markets. Although you may one day be interested in these more specialized trusts, you currently need to start with a broad, low-risk trust.

If you turn to the 'Investment Trust Categories' you'll find three 'International' categories, listed as 'General', 'Capital Growth' and 'Income'. There seems to be little difference in the returns from any of these categories, however – as generating a high income return is not your prime concern – you might wish to forget the 'International Income' category initially. This leaves you with two suitable investment categories: 'International General' and 'International Capital Growth', giving you a choice of over 40 investment trusts from which to choose.

Select one of the two categories and continue with the next step. By the way, it's worth doing the following steps with both categories in turn. There will undoubtedly be suitable trusts in both groups.

Step Three: Choose a Trust with Total Assets of Over £100 Million

Look for the 'Total Assets' column and cross off all those trusts that do not have total assets of over £100 million. This is where your ruler comes in handy. There are two reasons for choosing larger trusts initially: first, they tend to be the more established and relatively stable compared to newer smaller trusts. Secondly, the management charges are often lower in large trusts, where the management cost is borne by thousands of investors. You'll notice that some trusts have over £1 billion in total assets, while others may only have a market capitalization, as the professionals call it, of £30 million or less.

Step Four: Choose an Established Trust

Cross off any trusts that do not have a 10-year record. You'll be able to see this at a glance at 'Year 10' in the 'Share Price Total Return on £100' column, where there will be a dash instead of a share return indicated. (Make sure this is not as a result of insufficient information at time of printing, before you strike the trust off.) As this is your first investment, you are better with a well-established trust rather than a relatively young one.

Step Five: Choose a Broad Geographical Spread of Investments

Find the geographical spread, which also includes a cash and fixed interest column. Cross off any trusts that have over 70 per cent of their investments in any one of the geographical regions listed. This will ensure that your investments are not too reliant on any one market or country. In any case, you'll find that most trusts are broadly based and well under this 70 per cent threshold. Remember also that the UK stockmarket represents only about 5 per cent of the total world stockmarkets.

Step Six: Choose a High-performance Trust

You want to find out how each trust has performed in the last 10 years. You may have heard, time and again, that past performance is not necessarily a guide to future performance. This is of course undeniable; the future is always uncertain. However, when dealing with investment trusts a consistently good track record is often the best indicator for good performance in the future. So:

- Find the 'Share Price Total Return on £100' column. The simplest way to assess performance is to compare each trust with the average performance of the entire category. (Note that the figures in these columns represent the return from £100 invested. In other words, if you had invested £100 10 years ago, the amount listed in the 10-year column is how much your investment would be worth today.)

- Compare the return on £100 in each year for each trust with the size-weighted average return. Cross out any returns that are below the average. When you've done this for each trust, the top performers will automatically appear as those trusts where the yearly returns have consistently out-performed the average. Earmark those trusts that have performed best. Ideally, there should be trusts whose returns were all above average. If this is not the case in your selection, then opt for the next best thing: the trusts with only one return under average. Cross off all the other trusts that have under-performed.

Now compare each trust you've selected with the FTSE Actuaries All Share Index. How have they performed against this classic benchmark? If you find that the performance of your selected trusts is under the FTSE Index, then you might want to consider a 'tracker fund' – often considered a good investment trust to start with. The objective of this guide is to help you choose a trust that will perform *better* than the FTSE Index and produce a return that is at least

10 per cent *over* the Index. If performance is above that of the FTSE All Shares Index, then continue the selection process.

Note: Past performance is no certain guide to future performance. However, compare a trust that has performed better than average for the preceding 1, 3, 4 and 10 years with another trust that has performed below average over the same period. Which one would you entrust with your essential savings? The fact remains that consistently sound performance, while not a guarantee, is a better indicator than consistently poor performance.

Step Seven: Choose a Trust with a Good Net Asset Value Return [NAV]

- The share price indicates the market demand for the trust. Now look at the real underlying value of the trust. Often the share price return and the asset value return tend to reflect each other closely. You should find that a trust that is performing well also has a high net asset value return. But this is not always the case. You now need to repeat the elimination of those trusts that are producing a below average NAV return:

  Find the 'NAV total return on £100'. Cross off all returns that are below the size-weighted average.

  Now compare both the share return and NAV results. Earmark those trusts that have both an above-average share price return and net asset value return. These are your potential ideal trusts.

Step Eight: Choose a Suitable Saving Scheme

With the top trusts identified, you should now check whether the savings scheme on offer is acceptable. Most companies operate very similar conditions for their private investors, however there can be surprises; make sure that you haven't picked the one investment trust that requires a £5,000 minimum investment, or does not allow you to reinvest your dividend, or perhaps has particularly high transaction charges.

- Find out which investment companies manage your selected trusts by turning to the 'Management Information' listed further on in the AITC magazine. A typical savings scheme should have the following profile:

  Regular savings minimum monthly: £25–£50

  Lump sum minimum: £250–£500; sometimes £1,000

  Dividend reinvestment: Yes. This is essential in order to maximize the effect of compound growth. Choose a trust that will allow you to reinvest the dividend automatically. Also check that purchasing and selling shares can be done at minimal or no cost. Again, nearly all trusts allow you to do this at a reasonable charge. Some investment companies do not charge for purchasing or selling shares. Instead, they claim their charges directly from the trust as a management fee. (So you are still paying the charges, albeit in an indirect way.)

  Purchase and Selling Facility: Yes.

  Scheme Transaction Charges: These charges will depress your trust performance in the long term, and you really want to keep them as low as possible. Charges should be no more than 0.5 per cent to purchase or sell shares. Some investment companies appear to have no transaction charges. A 'nil' entry under 'scheme charges' simply means that the transaction charges are lumped together with a fee that the investment company charges the trust, in return for its management services. You will need to check the investment company brochure to find out what the exact transaction charges are before committing to a trust.

Annual Management Fee. The annual management fee will be listed in the individual investment company brochures. It should be no more than 0.7 per cent on your total savings placed in the trust. Total transaction and management fees should not exceed 1 per cent of your savings; consider crossing off any companies that are charging you 1 per cent or over. (You will notice that more specialized trusts do have higher charges of between 1 and 3 per cent, reflecting the higher cost of managing more complex investments.)

Optional PEP Schemes. Some investment companies offer PEPs at no additional (initial or annual) cost to the saving scheme offered. As long as there are no additional costs, these schemes are worth it – as you are benefiting from some tax relief on your Income Tax, without paying punitive charges normally associated with PEP schemes. Be careful, though, because some investment companies do charge considerable fees, often between 3 and 5 per cent if you choose to invest through a PEP. The marginal tax savings you'd make in a PEP would not justify paying these sorts of charges. As a simple rule: avoid PEP schemes unless they are offered at no additional cost than the normal management and transaction charges of the investment trust, in which case you may as well take advantage of the slight tax relief on income. (Remember that Capital Gains Tax is irrelevant to PEP-holders with less than £100,000 invested.)

- Cross off those trusts whose terms and conditions are unacceptable to you.

Step Nine: Order the Investment Companies' Brochures

By now you have a few trusts that are suitable for your Independence Fund savings. Before you make a final decision you must read through the brochures of the investment companies that manage these trusts. As well as finding out more about the background of the Investment Company, you should check for the more in-depth information, as there may be slight variances with what was reported in the AITC magazine. Remember to check:

- what the transaction charges are
- what the annual management fee is
- what the actual conditions of the savings scheme are
- whether a PEP can be taken out at no additional charge.

Step Ten: Make a Decision

Once you've read the investment company brochures, a particular company and trust may well stand out from the rest as your perfect choice. More often than not, this will not be the case and more than one trust will seem ideal for your Fund. You'd probably be right too; any trust that has survived your gruelling selection procedure this far is likely to be a good option for your Independence Fund.

Just think about it: a trust on your shortlist is sufficiently large and established, has broad world-wide global investments, an above-average performance, and operates a flexible and cost-effective savings scheme designed for you, the private investor. You have distilled an optimum route for creating your Independence Fund. Do not deliberate on minor details and remember that you can always change it at a later date.

So:

- Make your choice. Fill out the application form and Direct Debit instructions. Write out the cheque and post it all first class to the address given.

Congratulations, you've done it. Welcome to a new era and lifestyle.

SUMMARY

An ideal investment trust can be chosen using this checklist and a monthly report known as the *Monthly Information Service* published by the Association of Investment Trust Companies (AITC).

The selection of a trust involves:

- choosing an international trust
- eliminating any trusts that have less than £100 million in total assets, do not have a 10-year record and are not geographically diverse
- rating the remaining trusts on performance by comparing share price and net asset value return on savings
- opting for a suitable saving scheme, checking the management company brochures and taking a decision.

10 STARTING OUT

HOMEWORK

We left Kate's freshly painted flat with copies of the 'Starter Kit' firmly in our grasp. I thought that we'd call her up towards the end of the week and thank her for her help; maybe send her a card and perhaps let her know how we were getting on. Dan had other ideas: he was determined to see her again, and consequently he was determined to start his Fund as soon as possible.

He read the guide to finding a suitable investment trust that very evening. The next day, he took an hour off work to track down the AITC offices and obtain their monthly information brochure in person. The receptionist was so impressed with his eagerness that she gave him a couple of back issues. That night he shut himself in his room to read the magazine until midnight. By Wednesday morning Dan called his selected investment companies and insisted he needed to see their investment trust brochures as soon as possible. The company brochures arrived before the end of the week. On Friday morning, Dan rang Kate.

Kate was stunned. Barely a week had passed since we were painting her flat. Dan had sorted out his Independence Fund in record time. Moreover, he was asking some pertinent questions over the phone. She was impressed and agreed to meet up again at a local café to go over the final stage.

I'd been too distracted by events at work even to start my selection. Dan announced that he was meeting Kate on Saturday morning for a chat on his investment options. Not to worry if I was busy, he'd take notes of what she said and pass them on. I told him I'd definitely be coming too, and spent Friday evening working through Kate's guide, as if the meeting the following day was some sort of exam. Saturday morning found Dan barely able to suppress his enthusiasm at having followed through with Kate's guide. He declared it the 'first time I've fully understood anything remotely financial'.

CHOOSING A TRUST

'Have you chosen a trust yet?'

'Well, I've narrowed it down to three, but I can't decide beyond that. All three have above-average performances and very low charges; in fact, they're virtually identical.'

'I'm in the same situation,' I add. 'Is there any other criteria that we could consider to sway the decision one way or the other? What should we be looking for in the company brochures when they arrive?'

COMPANY BROCHURES

First of all, I wouldn't worry too much if you can't decide between trusts. As I mentioned in the 'Starter Kit', I'm sure any of the trusts that have survived the selection so far would be fine. But there are some secondary aspects that could sway the decision for you. One is the *quality of the information* in the investment company brochures. Some brochures are well written and easy to understand, while others can be very confusing and misleading.

Reading the investment trust brochure can help you to make a decision; one company sent more of a package than a brochure. It was so full of irrelevant performance appraisals, graphs and pie charts that it gave me a headache after half an hour. The more I read it, the less confident I was about investing. I took the wise decision to throw it in the bin and crossed that trust off my list. Whether it was intentional or not, I had the impression the company was complicating the process – which wasn't a good footing to start on. Fortunately, the other trusts I shortlisted had excellent brochures that were clear and succinct.

Use the brochures to check on the background details on a company. Look at its track record, how long it has been established for, the terms of its saving scheme, and of course what charges there are.

All this you need to cross-refer. You want to make sure that the trust has indeed been around for longer than the last 10 years, for example, or that the charge structure does not have any hidden extras that have gone hitherto unmentioned.

Do not pay much attention to performance claims made in the trusts. This is pure advertising – every trust can select a particular period within the last 20 years which shows it in the best possible light. It's far better to rely on impartial sources such as the AITC for this sort of information, where the relative performance figures speak for themselves. This is exactly what you will have done by choosing your trust with the help of the Starter Kit.

MANAGEMENT TEAM

The other aspect you could consider is the quality of the management team in your chosen trusts. There are articles in the investment magazines that profile the fund managers and set out their strategies, but you'd probably find it hard to assess the quality of a manager without knowing the business more intimately. However, you can look at how stable the management structure is. For example, is the fund manager or team that was responsible for the excellent performance over the last five years still there, or has he or she (or they) just moved elsewhere? This sort of information you can generally find in the annual reports.

PURCHASING SHARES 'AT A DISCOUNT' OR 'AT A PREMIUM'

The third aspect you could consider is whether the shares are at a discount or at a premium. You already know this has something to do with the net asset value (NAV) and the share pricing. It's actually the difference between the market value – or rather share price – and the value of the underlying investments. It's always expressed as a percentage in the AITC magazine. If the share price is higher than the NAV, the share is said to be 'at a premium', as investors will have to pay more than the underlying value of the share. Shares at a premium are in demand – in other words, investors are prepared to pay more than their 'real' current value. You might wonder why an investor would pay more than the real value for a share. Usually they're anticipating the share price will rise even further, and that therefore so will their return.

If a share is 'at a discount', it simply means that the net asset value is greater than what the market will bear – or pay for the share. It's always a question of supply and demand. Buying shares at a discount is beneficial to the investor as long as the shares eventually rise. You are buying at less than the real value of the assets of the trust. If shares are trading at a 10 per cent discount, for example, then £100 of investments can be purchased for £90.

At this level of investing, you shouldn't be overly concerned as to whether shares are at a premium or at a discount. It isn't that critical to your choice, but it is useful to keep in mind. It's more of an added bonus if you're buying shares at a discount when it appears the trust is going to do well. I'd only consider it as a last consideration, once you've sifted out your top trusts. It might help you decide if the trusts you've selected are very similar. Typically, you'd opt for the trust with the shares at a discount. It's very much an 'extra' consideration for you at the moment. It's much more important for the professionals, who of course will be comparing a multitude of other indicators at the same time before they make an investment decision. Or at least that's the theory.

HOW INTERNATIONAL DOES IT HAVE TO BE?

I've recommended you choose an international trust because it spreads your investment risk as widely as possible. You might have

noticed that the so-called international trusts have anything between 40 and 60 per cent of their investments in the United
Kingdom – which of course doesn't sound particularly international.

One of the reasons for this is certainly historical. As these are UK
trusts, it is somewhat inevitable that an international trust will have a
significant proportion of its investments in UK companies. This is a
market that the fund managers know well and are experienced in. If
you were to invest in North American Mutual Funds, which are the
American equivalent to investment trusts, you will undoubtedly find
that the large, broad low-risk funds will have a significant number of
American companies in their portfolio.

Bear in mind also that investment portfolios are not static entities.
A fund manager's investment strategy will vary according to the state
of the stockmarket. Fund managers might be investing 'aggressively'
or 'defensively', depending on their perceptions of the stockmarkets.
A collapse in one stockmarket will lead fund managers to invest in
another – the UK for example, where the lower susceptibility to currency fluctuations is an added bonus. So is a 60 per cent investment
in one country too high for an international trust? The answer would
have to be no. I wouldn't be overly preoccupied with it. However, if all
other factors were equal I would lean towards a trust that had less
than 50 per cent in any one region or country.

WHAT ABOUT THE OTHER CATEGORIES OF
INVESTMENT TRUST?

If you've been examining the AITC investment service carefully,
you're probably wondering why you don't invest in another investment trust category that happens to be performing better than the
international trust category at present. It comes down to risk again –

although I'll be the first to admit that the American and European markets are large, mature and usually good investment material. I wouldn't be overly concerned if you chose an American or European trust as opposed to an international one, but you should bear in mind that it will be more susceptible to the highs and lows of those respective markets. All is well now, but who knows what may happen in 5 or 10 years. Nothing stops you from investing in any category of investment trust. Taking out an international trust reduces your risk of a slump in any one market. You only need to look at events in Japan and the Far East in 1998 to appreciate this. Few experts were able to predict this 10 years ago – or even two years before it happened. I would still recommend an international trust as your starting point.

WHAT ABOUT A US MUTUAL FUND?

There are two substantial drawbacks to this approach for a UK investor. First, you'll have US tax complications, which are not worthwhile for a starter Fund. Secondly, you'll have to invest in dollars and this means an extra charge every month for converting from pounds Sterling to US dollars. Paying an exchange charge to Thomas Cook for holiday money is one thing, but paying exchange charges on your Independence Fund is another. Once your Fund has grown substantially, you might want to consider investing through US Mutual Funds, but forget it as a starting option.

Dan has been trying to attract the waitress for the last few minutes, to no avail. He shrugs as she disappears yet again. I look down at his papers. He has prepared two sheets of questions, which he's been ticking off as we talk. Completely out of character for him to have prepared anything in his life, apart from a few meals. But Kate wouldn't appreciate this, of course, having only known him for a week.

'So, Jon, how did you find the selection of your trust?'

'Fine until I had to start reading the investment company brochures – I'm in the same situation as Dan, I can't decide between a few trusts, although after what you've just said I will have another look at them.'

'Have you two compared which trusts you've chosen?'

'That would be cheating!' Dan frowns. 'I'm not going to let Jon see my choicest trusts.'

'We're trying to see if we end up choosing the same one.' I explain. 'If we don't, we're going to have bets on whose trust performs the best. It'll be an annual event and the loser will have to buy the other a bottle of whisky, do the washing up, cook a meal and polish the other's shoes.'

'As if an annual return isn't reward enough,' Kate says, shaking her head.

THE INVESTOR STRATEGY

An element to the Starter Kit that has confused would-be investors is the fact that it recommends you choose an investment trust that has a consistent share value and is already performing well. I used to be under the impression, from the little I knew about investing at the time, that a good investor always looked for shares that were doing badly or under-performing. The idea seemed to be that you bought shares at a substantial discount so that you made a significant profit when the share price rose again. The approach I recommend does exactly the opposite of this. The Starter Kit guides you to look for consistent value rather than trying to find a trust that has been under-performing.

Significant gains can be made from speculating and purchasing shares at a significant discount in the anticipation that they will rise. The key element to success is that your shares do in fact rise as antici-pated. It can be highly lucrative, but it is riskier as you are speculating on what the market will do. This type of investing requires you to pro-vide three basic ingredients: an avid interest in investing, spare time, and non-essential funds. Speculating will require much more involve-ment on your part. You do not want to start experimenting with your Independence Fund. So this is not really an option for a beginner.

MOVING ON

'And you won't regret it. You should be able to go back to your trusts and choose one now. Shall we move on to the last thing we have to discuss?'

'How to maintain the Fund?'

'That's right.'

'And how to spend our Fund without stuffing it up – which has to be the most important part of all,' Dan adds.

'Of course – how could I forget.'

SUMMARY

These are the secondary considerations that must be considered prior to deciding on an investment trust. Some aspects may help you to make a final decision. They include:

- the quality and clarity of the information in the company brochures
- the experience of the fund manager and management team
- whether shares are 'at a premium' or 'at a discount'
- the importance of choosing a broad international trust in the early years.

US Mutual Funds are not an ideal investment route for someone starting an Independence Fund, given the tax and currency complications.

The Starter Kit shows how a suitable trust can be selected on the basis of consistent performance and a sound return on investment, as opposed to the more speculative approach some people might associate with investing in general.

11 MAKING IT WORK

'What are you having?' Dan asks as the waitress appears.
Kate and I order coffee. Dan opts for a camomile tea.
Something is definitely up with him today. I let the moment
pass, though.

'So, where were we?' I ask.

'Kate is about to tell us how we can spend our savings.'

'No I'm not, Dan. That's the last thing you need help with.
Before you start spending any of the Fund, you'd better find
out how to ensure it accumulates properly.'

'All right. So how do we maximize our independence savings then?'

MAXIMIZING THE FUND

MATCH YOUR PAYMENTS WITH YOUR EARNINGS

When you receive a salary rise, increase your contributions to the trust. If you receive a bonus from work, put 10 per cent into your Fund. But don't struggle to meet the payments into your trust if your income has collapsed or if you have large emergency bills to pay. You should accelerate the Fund when you can afford to, but if times are hard you do not want an additional burden. Making the contributions proportional to your real earnings is important to the Fund's 'sustainability'.

What happens if you stop work for a while? Maybe you've left your job or it is the end of a contract. If you're without an income, stop the contributions into the trust but keep a note on how many payments you've missed. When you do begin earning again, try and make up the difference. That might be difficult to do in some cases, but if you've only stopped working for a couple of months, then you could easily increase the subsequent payments slightly to compensate.

If you're having problems making contributions into the Fund for whatever reason, then you should perhaps reduce the amount you put in. Try and avoid stopping the payments completely, because regular investing works in your favour, as you know. Use the 10 per cent guideline as a rule of thumb and adjust accordingly.

Invariably there will be times when you find it difficult to keep up your independence savings, such as if you're starting a family. At times like this, bear in mind that you need to tailor your savings to what you can realistically afford, irrespective of the rule of thumb. Remember that you can increase the payments or lower them according to your financial situation, which is likely to change over the years. Of course, if you're sustaining the Fund properly, your financial situation will certainly change for the better.

REINVEST THE DIVIDEND

The second detail you must remember – and I only bring it up because I forgot to do this when I first started out – is to give instructions to the Management Company of your trust that you want your dividend payments reinvested automatically. Normally there's a box you have to tick on the application form.

MONITOR THE FUND

Now that you've chosen an ideal trust, you need to ensure that it remains an optimum environment for your Fund. The trust you chose could prove to be an excellent choice for the next 20 years, or it could begin to perform poorly after only a couple of years. Monitoring your chosen trust and being able to recognize how it is performing is critical to your Fund's success. Thankfully, it isn't that complicated.

The simplest check you can do on a regular basis is to repeat the steps outlined in the 'Starter Kit'. Obviously, you need an up-to-date AITC *Monthly Information Service* magazine. You'll probably have to pay for this one. Repeat the selection of an ideal trust and see where your Fund ends up. Is it still in the top three, or has it slipped to an average position?

If it is still in the top few that you've selected, then don't change anything. If you see it has dropped down and is lingering around the

FTSE Index, don't panic either. Shares will go up and down – it's a fact of life. Content yourself in the knowledge that you will be buying shares at a discount, and because you are purchasing them at regular monthly intervals you will be taking advantage of fixed cost averaging – which works in your favour, of course. In a market slump you have nothing to worry about unless you *have* to draw out funds, in which case it could be disastrous. Bear in mind that the market is cyclical; it typically rises but there will be setbacks, and sometimes sharp ones. Don't be overly concerned if your share prices drop. What is the general state of the market? If all the other trusts are experiencing a similar drop in value and share price, then don't worry. It's a market slump and should correct itself. Remember you are a long-term investor, and provided you aren't in urgent need of your savings, then there isn't much to panic about. It may be alarming to see your trust sink by 10 per cent, until you realize that all the other trusts have dropped by 30 per cent.

TAKE ACTION

On the other hand, what do you do when it is only your trust that has sunk well below the average? Or you find that your trust is consistently under-performing over 24 months?

For a start, try and find out why it is happening in your trust. Read the company reports, which should be sent to you every six months. An ideal time to check your trust performance is at the end of the financial year, when you can read the annual report in conjunction with the AITC and other magazines. Inform yourself as to why the share price has dropped. There could be a very good reason, and you might be confident enough with your trust not to move your savings. Perhaps there's been a slight change in investment strategy that will be beneficial in the long term. On the other hand, you do not want to be clinging to a trust that is going to do badly for the next five years.

Above all, keep it in context. Think of football. In selecting your investment trust you've chosen the equivalent of a top Premier Division team. What are their chances of being relegated to the First Division? Fairly remote, unless something goes seriously wrong, in which case you'll be able to foresee it. Your trust performance will be similar. Provided you're checking the performance of your trust once or twice a year, you will have advance notice of whether you should make changes or not.

'Let's see if I have this right,' says Dan, leaning forward on his chair and looking at his notes. 'So we check our trust. If we find it's still performing above average, we leave it alone. If it has slipped down to average performance, we don't worry about that either. But if it slips below the average and doesn't show any sign of recovering, then we take action; we should select another trust that is performing well and transfer our funds over.'

'Yes, that's right,' Kate answers. 'And if the market is particularly unsettled you might want to choose a tracker fund to be safe. This is where you'll appreciate low entry and exit charges. You'll not be charged much if you decide to transfer your savings to another trust.'

'Right, I see.' Dan ticks his list as the waitress delivers two coffees and the camomile tea. All image, of course – Dan is the unhealthiest bloke I know.

KEEP AWARE

The Government has been encouraging individuals and families to start their own pension and savings schemes for years, and this trend is expected to continue apace. New schemes may well be introduced that offer the individual an alternative investment route for the Independence Fund. You need to at least be aware of such new developments and their potential implications on your independence savings. One can only hope that any new tax-relief schemes will be significant improvements on the current ones.

HOW TO USE THE FUND

MISUSE

As you watch the Fund accumulate, the temptation might arise to use it for trivialities now, rather than save it for a time when you will really need it. The Fund relies entirely on your own self-discipline and judgement as to how it should be used. This is both its strength and weakness. Avoid the temptation to misuse the Fund, especially in its early years. You don't want to see the Independence Fund become insignificant through persistent use – or rather, abuse. The best way to remain objective about its use is to clarify when the independence savings should or could be used.

JUSTIFIABLE USE

Justifiable uses that come to mind include:

- to finance a career change: the Fund can be used to
  provide a supplementary income when changing careers, or

if you've been made redundant. Alternatively, you might wish to return to study, take a course to obtain new skills, or face a costly relocation to a new town. This 'bridging finance' allows you to change career direction or to provide a financial breather until you are earning an income once more.

- reasonable downpayment on a house or flat: we've already mentioned how the savings can be used to meet the downpayment on a home. This can be regarded as an investment alternative.

- emergencies: the Independence Fund is obviously available in the event of a crisis where funds are required urgently. Only an individual can determine what *really* constitutes an 'emergency'.

- to supplement your income: your income may drop as a result of a career change, retirement, disability or whatever. Income from the fund could be used to ease the transition to perhaps a less frenetic or demanding lifestyle. It could even be used later on to buy an annuity – although this would be unusual.

'So, a Sony Play Station's out of the question?' asks Dan.

'You are joking, I hope. I can't think of anything less appropriate.'

'That's all right, I'm more of an outdoor bloke anyway,' Dan lies.

'Mind you,' Kate adds. 'There may be other uses, but they'll come down to individual preferences and pressures; for example, paying university fees could be another potential use for your savings, too.'

'Fine. I'm sure we can come up with other ways to spend the Fund too. How do we withdraw our savings out of the Fund? You mentioned there was a way to do this without adversely affecting the Fund's long-term growth. Is that still possible?'

HOW TO WITHDRAW FUNDS

There are two ways to draw out savings without harming the overall growth of the Fund: If you've left your savings untouched for years, then you might be able to live off the dividends it produces without damaging the core amount in your Fund. Of course, we're looking at 10 or 20 years' growth before you can start living off the income effectively.

Otherwise, if the Fund is still 'immature', then you could borrow from it. Consider your Independence Fund as your own personal bank and treat any withdrawal from your Fund as a personal loan that you have to pay back. When you need additional funds to make an emergency purchase, this is what you should do:

- Decide on how much you need to take out.
- Contact a bank and ask them for a *personal loan proposal* for the amount that you wish to withdraw from your Fund.
- 'Borrow' this amount from your Independence Fund.
- Repay the amount you borrowed and the interest due by using the repayment schedule provided by the bank.

This system of borrowing and repaying at the current market rates will ensure that your Fund still grows effectively over time. Repaying the Fund using a bank repayment schedule will compensate the

Fund for the loss of the savings you withdrew. You can exercise some discretion as well. If you are not earning a sufficient amount to repay over a year or so, you can stretch the repayment out to suit yourself. Tell the bank you'd like an example of a five-year repayment proposal, and adjust your repayments accordingly. If your income improves, you can pay it off sooner. Either way, you are gradually returning the savings plus interest into the Fund, and the net effect of this is to sustain your Fund's long-term growth.

If you simply repay the amount borrowed six months later without interest, you will have lost out on six months of capital growth on that money.

'Have you done this, Kate?'

'I have. I needed a computer and printer to start my freelance work. I couldn't afford it without dipping into my Fund, which had only been started 18 months previous. I used this repayment system, and gradually paid back the full amount, so the net effect on my Fund was minimal. It has still grown phenomenally well.'

'Did you contact the bank to find out how much to repay?'

'Not in that case. I shopped around for the best "cash deal" I could find and then told the shop manager that I'd be paying it in instalments and could they provide me with a hire-purchase repayment schedule. A word of warning: some shops advertise interest-free purchase schemes. Don't believe them. This is usually a marketing ploy and the interest is virtually always factored into the price shown.'

'That doesn't surprise me.'

'So I took the shop repayment scheme and used it to pay back my loan to the Independence Fund. The interest payable on the hire purchase agreement was 16 per cent, which is not a bad return for the Independence Fund. That's how I managed to keep the Fund accumulating. The interest was compensating for any lost capital growth.'

A MATURE FUND

What happens when the Fund grows up? What happens when you've accumulated over £100,000? Should you seriously start thinking about tax relief? Does the size of the Fund mean that you need to manage it in a different way?

ALLOW SAVINGS TO ACCUMULATE

First of all, if your investment route is performing well, leave your savings alone. Don't start moving the funds about in search of an even better investment trust on a whim. You do not want to pay transfer charges – however reasonable they are – without good reason. Provided your chosen trust is consistently in the upper quartile, then stay where you are.

DIVERSIFY YOUR INVESTMENT

When your Fund has grown to between £50,000 and £100,000, then you may be inclined to look at diversification – that is, placing some savings into another trust. Splitting the trust in this way will lessen your investment risk further. The easiest option is to choose other trusts that match the optimal criteria listed. Alternatively, you might feel confident enough to try another category of trust.

Broad trusts such as a North American or European trust might be suitable.

On the other hand, you might opt for a specialized trust that invests in a specific region or industry. Bear in mind that a specialized trust might incur higher charges and a higher investment risk, but if you're investing in an area such as 'high technology', the returns could be impressive. If you do diversify your investments be aware that some specialized trusts invest in unlisted companies, which makes it difficult to assess their real asset value objectively. Unlisted companies are not valued daily on the stockmarket; the valuation is left to the fund managers, and this sometimes leads to inaccurate or misleading indications on the true value of a holding. If you can't be bothered to spend more time on your investment, then just choose another general trust that is performing well.

AVOID THE TAX ZONE

By the time your total funds reach about £100,000, you are starting to face potential Capital Gains Tax liabilities. Your personal Capital Gains Tax allowance is currently £6,800 a year, but this allowance tends to rise according to the Retail Price Index. With increased exposure to tax, a PEP begins to look more attractive and savings will begin to outweigh the charges associated with a PEP.

'What about the ISA, though?' I ask.

'Unfortunately, not much is known about the ISA. It is meant to replace the PEP, but the details have yet to be finalized and we can only hope it will have a favourable impact on personal savings and investments. With any luck, it will be less restrictive than the PEP and offer real tax relief without the

*usual associated charges that these schemes seem to attract,'
Kate replies, taking a sip of her coffee.*

*'Only time will tell, I suppose,' I say, watching Dan write this
down.*

*'Do you know, I think we've almost finished our financial
induction?' Kate says, leaning back. 'Although perhaps there
is one last point.'*

'Let me guess. You're going to charge us a commission?'

'If only.'

POTENTIAL ALTERNATIVE ROUTES

The final point is that investment trusts may not always be the optimal solution for your investment. Legislation changes all the time,
and the financial industry responds by adapting its products to the
new circumstances. Invariably, charges and commissions are built
into the schemes. There are a number of tax incentives and relief that
could be extended to the individual.

One could be to allow gross income contributions into an Independence Fund. Another could be to extend tax relief to capital and
income gains while personal savings remain invested. While a tax on
funds withdrawn may be reasonable, too many restrictions on how
these savings are used would be unwieldy. Such tax relief could better equip people to become more self-reliant and less dependent on
the state for temporary income, retraining, or other benefits. A tax-free
Independence Fund could make a dramatic difference to an individual
– provided, of course, that there are no excessive associated charges.

A number of events can happen that could alter the optimal
environment for your Fund. The chances are that it will remain an

equity-linked scheme, but I don't know whether it will always be an investment trust. As I'm aware of this and because I don't want to mislead you in anyway, I've drafted a checklist that will help you to appraise any new schemes that you come across.

THAT'S IT!

'Well, you now know as much as I do, more or less,'
Kate says.

'I don't believe that for a second, but thank you all the same. You've revolutionized my entire financial understanding,' I say, and I mean every word.

'Not that surprising considering where we started off from,' Dan points out. 'Kate, you do realize that we'll be calling you up whenever we need the slightest bit of financial advice from now on.'

'That's fine – just be aware that there's a commission from now on. We're staying for lunch, aren't we?'

'Definitely. Jon's offered to pay,' Dan volunteers.

'Oh, that's kind. Will you excuse me for a moment? I'll just make a phone call.' We watch Kate weave between the tables to the phone on the bar counter. Dan is mesmerized again.

'Talk about return on capital,' he says, beaming.

'Wake up, Dan.'

'Well, nothing ventured – nothing gained. You can't reap a high return until you've made the initial investment. You should know that by now.'

SUMMARY

Once the Fund is set up, your financial independence is within reach provided that you:

- make regular contributions that are proportional to earnings and prove sustainable in the long term
- ensure dividends are reinvested for maximum growth
- monitor the Fund's performance and take appropriate action if performance slips
- remain aware of changes in industry practice and Government legislation
- only use the Fund for genuine reasons:
- to finance a career change
- as a reasonable downpayment on home
- as a supplement to your income
- for an emergency
- withdraw from the Fund using a 'borrow and repay' scheme that will not damage its long-term growth.

As the Fund matures, an investor should begin to consider:

- diversifying investments
- saving schemes that minimize taxes
- new investment routes as and when they are introduced.

KATE'S IDEAL CHECKLIST

The only guarantee that can be made of the future is that it will be different. This is equally true of the investment world. This checklist has been written so that you can make an objective assessment of new investment routes and their potential as 'optimal environments' for the Independence Fund. Used in conjunction with the Starter Kit, this checklist should help you determine whether or not a potential investment route is indeed suitable. The *ideal* answer to each question is YES, although a YES to all is highly unlikely. If you do find a route which satisfies all the following questions – let us know about it!

- Does the investment you are considering have a track record?

- Has it been in existence for over 10 years?

- Do the managers of the investment have a good public record? Has the managing company been implicated in any unethical investments or business practices? Has it been involved in pension mis-selling, for example?

- Has the net asset value of the investment out-performed the FTSE Index regularly over the last 10 years?

- Has the share price been better than the FTSE Index over the last 10 years?

- Is the investment fund large enough to keep management costs down to an acceptable level? (at least £100 million for a trust)

- Are you buying at an advantageous price (or discount)?

- Can you check the value of your investment easily?

- Is the geographical location of the investment(s) acceptable to you?

- Does the literature and information about the investment make sense to *you*?

- Is it economic and convenient to invest small amounts regularly?

- Are management fees and carrying charges competitive and acceptable to you? Are they (ideally) under 1 per cent of the total invested?

- Are transaction charges on purchases and sales acceptable? Are they under a half per cent of the total amount sold or invested?

- Can dividends be automatically reinvested?

- Is your investment free of onerous transaction charges or penalties if you switch?

- Can you sell easily and quickly if you have to, and without incurring a penalty?

- Can you borrow on your investment if you need to?

- Can you invest gross income – that is, before deduction of income tax?

- Can income and capital gains be sheltered from taxation?

- Are you free to use the funds realized for any purpose?

- Are you free of any contractual obligations?

- Are you making a conscious decision to make the investment yourself? Are you definitely not being 'sold' the idea?

- Can you sustain this rate of investment on a regular basis? Can you afford the monthly payment?

FURTHER INFORMATION AND RESOURCES

A DEDICATED WEBSITE

If you would like further information specifically on the Independence Fund, then have a look at www.getsorted.co.uk, which is dedicated to bringing you updates on aspects that will affect your independence savings.

This website will keep you posted on any changes in legislation or industry practice that will affect you and your Fund. You are also welcome to ask questions about any ideas raised in this book – and we will endeavour to reply!

OTHER SOURCES

Here is a list of other sources that you might wish to refer to, should you be looking for further information:

MAGAZINES

AITC *Monthly Information Service*

This monthly magazine is published by the Association of Investment Trust Companies (AITC) and seems to be the bible of the industry. It is available on subscription, though single 'sample' copies are available directly from the Association at: Durrant House, 8 Chiswell Street, London EC1 4YY (tel. 0171–282 5555; email: info@aitc.co.uk)

While the data is presented in a rather drab manner, it *is* independent and serves as the authoritative source on investment trusts in the United Kingdom. The AITC also published some very helpful pamphlets on various aspects of investment trusts, which are available at no cost. Investment trust performance details for up to 10 years are provided.

Investors Chronicle

This is a weekly magazine used extensively by the investment community. In addition to commenting regularly on individual investment trusts, the *Investors Chronicle* publishes an annual survey of the industry with performance details given for up to five years for each of trusts covered.

Investment Trust Magazine

A monthly magazine available on the newsstand or by subscription that focuses on investment trusts – as the name suggests. There is some useful anecdotal information on management teams, fund manager profiles and respective strategies. It is also fairly easy to read for newcomers to the investment world.

Other Magazines

There are many other magazines that deal with the broader spectrum of personal finances and sometimes have feature articles on investment trusts. None of these can be regarded as essential reading, however, and some tend to appear on the shelves and fade away with regularity. The more stable magazines are *Personal Finance*, *Money Management*, and *Which? Mortgage*.

August Issue of *Forbes* (US publication)

This is an authoritative magazine that devotes the *August issue* every year to a comprehensive survey of US Mutual Funds, the equivalent of our own Unit and Investment Trusts. This magazine provides penetrating research into the industry and is worth studying if you are seriously considering US Mutual Funds.

Wiesenberger (US publication)

This is a comprehensive annual directory of US Mutual Funds and is indispensable to the professional investor with shares in the American market. One of the funds chosen by the author using this directory in 1966 has grown at the rate of 17 per cent per annum ever since!

NEWSPAPERS

Many of the daily and weekend papers have good, easy to understand articles on investment trusts. The *Mail on Sunday* has particularly good 'general purpose' articles. Remember that there are restrictions on the amount of advertising that investment trusts can make as compared to unit trusts, for example. Do not be surprised if there is far more newspaper coverage and many more advertisements on unit trusts. Don't forget who ends up paying for it all, either.

BOOKS

If you've ever ventured into the financial section of a bookshop (usually it's right at the back near the emergency fire exit) then you were probably surprised by the vast array of books that have been written about personal finances. Banks, building societies and life insurance companies sponsor a good number of these. Their primary aim is to generate publicity, of course, and we believe many of these books are of questionable objectivity. However, there are some impartial sources available:

The Daily Mail Savers Guide

This is a comprehensive guide to most of the different types of investment available in the UK. It is useful as a basic reference and is updated annually. Investment Trust Saving Schemes are covered succinctly but fairly.

Get a Financial Life: Personal finances in your twenties and thirties by Beth Kobliner (New York: Simon & Schuster, 1996)

This is an American bestseller, which covers almost everything a young person would want to know about personal finance. Much of the book is applicable also to the UK, although the US terminology could well put many readers off.

How to Fix Your Finances: A guide to personal financial planning by Stephen Lofthouse (Chichester: Wiley, 1996)

An excellent and comprehensive guide to personal and financial planning, with a good chapter on investment trusts. This book is attractively written, well researched and a good reference manual for private investors.

Complete Guide to Investment Trusts (published by the AITC)

This is a weighty directory describing all the trusts available in the UK. It is primarily of interest to professional advisors. There are some helpful general articles.

Saving for Your Retirement by Eric Short (Bloomsbury, 1992)

A clear guide on a difficult subject. Balanced and objective, despite being published by a life insurance company.

We felt that the *Which?* guide, *Getting the best deal for your money*, was rather disappointing in its treatment of investment trusts.

OTHER WEBSITES

The World Wide Web is invariably becoming a good source of current information on investing, given the ongoing changes in investment markets, products and Government legislation.

Some websites are designed primarily to publicize financial companies, products and investment options and are of limited value to the investor seeking impartial advice. One site that does offer useful impartial advice aimed at the private investor is the Motley Fool, at www.fool.com. You might also like to browse through the following sites:

- www.find.co.uk
- www.iii.co.uk
- www.infotrade.co.uk
- www.moneyworld.co.uk
- www.trustnet.co.uk